D1491955

THE CHANGING LAW

AUSTRALIA
The Law Book Co. of Australasia Pty Ltd.
Sydney : Melbourne : Brisbane

CANADA AND U.S.A.
The Carswell Company Ltd.
Toronto

INDIA
N. M. Tripathi Ltd.
Bombay

NEW ZEALAND
Legal Publications Ltd.
Wellington

PAKISTAN
Pakistan Law House
Karachi

THE
CHANGING LAW

BY

THE RIGHT HONOURABLE

SIR ALFRED DENNING

*One of the Lords Justices of Her Majesty's
Court of Appeal in England*

LONDON

STEVENS & SONS LIMITED

1953

First published in 1953 by
Stevens & Sons Limited
of 119 & 120 Chancery Lane
London - Law Publishers
and printed in Great Britain
by The Eastern Press Ltd.
of London and Reading

CONTENTS

CONTENTS

PREFACE

WHEN I found recently that I had committed myself to deliver a number of addresses at our Universities, I thought it would be a good thing to make them with a common theme. This little book is the result. It is made up of the Foundation Oration at University College, London; the Haldane Memorial Lecture at Birkbeck College, London; addresses at The Law Society in London, at Oxford University and at Trinity College, Dublin; and the Earl Grey Memorial Lecture at the University of Durham. The book is not intended to be an exposition of legal propositions. It is only an attempt to draw a picture of the changes that are taking place. The reason for the title *The Changing Law* is because so many people think that the law is certain and that it can only be changed by Parliament. The truth is that the law is often uncertain and it is continually being changed, or perhaps I should say developed, by the judges. In theory the judges do not make law. They only expound it. But as no one knows what the law is until the judges expound it, it follows that they make it.

This process of gradual change has been the very life of the common law. The legal profession has usually found itself divided into two camps, those who want to make a change and those who prefer things to stay as they are; and between the two, we have somehow usually found the happy mean. To those who prefer no change, I would remark that when Lord Coke wrote his Reports (which were really textbooks) he was much criticised by the authorities on the ground that there were " many extravagant and exorbitant opinions set down and published for positive and good law," and he was ordered to expunge such " novelties and errors and offensive conceits as were dispersed in them." Yet Lord Coke so staked out the common law as to make it fit to control the course of the community for the next 150 years. Later on Lord Mansfield was bitterly attacked by Junius on the ground that " instead of those certain and positive rules by which the judgments of a court of law should invariably be determined, you have fondly introduced your own unsettled notions of equity and substantial justice." Yet Lord Mansfield so laid the foundations of our commercial law as to make it fit to control the commerce of the world. With these examples before us, we should not regard the common law as having the same characteristics as the law of the Medes and Persians. If the common law is to retain its place as the greatest system of law that the world has ever seen, it cannot stand still whilst everything else moves on. It must develop too. It must adapt itself to the new conditions. In these lectures I have tried to show how this is being done.

A. T. DENNING.

London,
    May, 1953.

THE SPIRIT OF THE BRITISH CONSTITUTION

" THE history of England is emphatically the history of progress. It is the history of a constant movement of the public mind, of a constant change in the constitutions of a great society." [1]   The last century has seen as great changes as any of the preceding centuries. There has been a social revolution accompanied by a constitutional revolution. When Dicey wrote in 1885 he could point to the sovereignty of parliament and to the rule of law as cardinal features of our constitution. Now, when we are more than half-way through the twentieth century, the emphasis has altogether changed.   In legal theory Parliament is still sovereign, and we still claim to be under the rule of law: but anxiety is raised in many quarters by the growing powers of the executive. The change has no doubt been forced upon us by circumstances. You cannot fight great wars except by giving your leaders power to make great decisions and to translate them into immediate action. You cannot safeguard your currency and trade in a competitive world except by strict control over exchange, and over exports and imports. You cannot ensure fair distribution of necessaries which are in short supply except by a system of rationing. You cannot nationalise essential industries except by putting them under the general direction of the Government. All this involves the entrusting of great powers to the executive: and the powers, once given, are apt to continue indefinitely. Some, indeed, have been made permanent: and others cannot be retracted.

[1] Macaulay's Essay on the History of the Revolution.

But, with all this change, nevertheless the spirit of the
constitution remains the same.   What is this spirit?
Like other things of the spirit, it is more easy to recognise
than to define.   It is to be felt rather than to be seen:
and to be experienced rather than to be learnt.   It is an
atmosphere which springs out of our long experience and
tradition.   If you would catch something of it, you should
go to Westminster Hall and remember the great scenes
that have been enacted there.   " The great hall of
William Rufus, the hall which has resounded with the
acclamations at the inauguration of thirty Kings . . . the
hall which witnessed the just sentence of Bacon and the
just absolution of Somers . . . the hall where Charles con-
fronted the High Court of Justice with the placid courage
which has half redeemed his fame . . . the hall where the
great proconsul Warren Hastings presented himself to his
Judges." [2]   Such memories will bring back to you some
of the great constitutional issues which have been decided
by the English people.   But you should also remember
that, in this hall for nigh on seven hundred years, the
judges of England laid down the common law which
precisely defined the rights of the individual and made
the life and liberty of every law-abiding citizen secure
from injury on the part of others or of the State.   Here
sat the judges of England right from the days of King
Henry II in 1189 till the year 1873 when the courts were
moved to their present situation in the Strand.   The
principles laid down by them have sunk deep into the
mind of the nation and have been more powerful than
anything else in creating the spirit of the British constitution.   If you reflect on all this in that hall, so strong and
so well balanced, so built as if for all time, you will get
a sense of wonderful history, and with it a knowledge that
the English people—and their cousins throughout the

[2] Macaulay's Essay on Warren Hastings.

British Commonwealth—are heirs of a spiritual worth which is a greater power in the world than armies or navies or atomic bombs.

THE THREE INSTINCTS

Again, however, I revert to the question, what is this spirit? It lies I believe, first, in the instinct for justice which leads us to believe that right, and not might, is the true basis of society; and secondly, in the instinct for liberty, which leads us to believe that free-will, and not force, is the true basis of government. These instincts for justice and liberty are abstract ideas which are common to all freedom-loving countries: but the peculiar genius of the British constitution lies in a third instinct, which is a practical instinct leading us to balance rights with duties, and powers with safeguards, so that neither rights nor powers shall be exceeded or abused. Throughout all this runs the Christian instinct and with it a sense of the supreme importance of the individual and a refusal to allow his personality to be submerged in an omnipotent State. This is in direct contrast to those constitutions which attach supreme importance to the State and little or none to the individual.

THE INSTINCT FOR JUSTICE

The first instinct, the instinct for justice, finds its expression in the rule of law. In order that right, and not might, should be the basis of society, the people must be under the rule of law, and there are four fundamental requisites which the law must fulfil: (1) it must be certain so that the people may act safely upon it; (2) it must be just so that they will approve of its being enforced; (3) it must be readily ascertainable, so that they may know what their rights and duties are; (4) it must be enforced by independent and upright judges in whom the people have confidence.

THE INDEPENDENCE OF THE JUDGES

The keystone of the rule of law in England has been the independence of the judges. It is the only respect in which we make any real separation of powers. There is here no rigid separation between the legislative and the executive powers: because the Ministers, who exercise the executive power, also direct a great deal of the legislative power of Parliament. But the judicial power is truly separate. The judges for the last 250 years have been absolutely independent. And when I speak of judges, I include not only the High Court judges, but also all the magistrates and others who exercise judicial functions. No member of the Government, no member of Parliament, and no official of any Government Department, has any right whatever to direct or to influence or to interfere with the decisions of any of the judges. It is the sure knowledge of this that gives the people their confidence in the judges—and I would add also the chairmen of tribunals when they are independent of the executive, for then they too are judges. It does not depend on the name " judge " or " chairman " but on the substance. The critical test which they must pass if they are to receive the confidence of the people is that they must be independent of the executive.

Why do the English people feel so strongly about this ? It is because it is born in them. We know in our bones that it will not do for us to allow the executive to have any control over the judges: and we know it because our forefathers learnt it in their struggles with the kings of England—the kings who in the old days exercised the supreme executive power in the land. Ever since the Act of Settlement in 1701 it has been part of our constitution that a judge of the High Court cannot be removed except for misconduct, and, even then, there must be a petition from both Houses of Parliament for his removal.   This means that a judge is virtually irremovable.   No judge has ever been dismissed from that time to this.   Secure from any fear of removal, the judges of England do their duty fearlessly, holding the scales evenly, not only between man and man, but also between man and the State.   Every judge on his appointment takes an oath that he " will do right to all manner of people according to the laws and customs of England, without fear or favour, affection or ill-will."   Never since 1701 has any judge failed to keep that oath.

THE CERTAINTY OF THE LAW

If the independence of the judges is the keystone, then the certainty and justice of the law is the structure on which the rule of law depends.   This certainty and justice is not attained in England by any code of laws.   The law of England was in former times for the most part declared by the judges, who were guided by the precedents of their predecessors.   They decided each case as justice demanded and then built up principles from the individual cases.   The precedents were collected and reported, and form a body of case-law unique in the history of the world.   The principles which they enunciated are still today the basis of our fundamental freedoms.   Our freedom of the Press, freedom of mind and conscience, and freedom of speech are all protected by the rules of law laid down by the judges.   To our mind this form of protection is better than the provisions of a written constitution.   Some may think that the English went too far in their adherence to precedent but it made for certainty, which has recently been described by Lord Simonds as of " paramount importance " in the law.[3] If the law so declared was found to be unjust or unsuited to changing times, it could only be altered by Parliament. The conception, however, of English law as being mainly judge-made law is out of date. Much more law is nowadays made by Parliament and by the Ministers than by the judges. The appellate courts of today do not spend much time in developing common law principles. They spend most of their time interpreting statutes made by Parliament or regulations made by Ministers. This does not, however, mean that there is any derogation from the rule of law itself. It does not matter so much who makes the law, the judges or the ministers, so long as it is certain, and just, and readily ascertainable by the people, or at any rate by their lawyers. Nor does it matter so much who tries the cases, whether it be judges or tribunals, so long as they are independent of the executive. These are the only principles which are involved in the rule of law and they have over the centuries become part of the British constitution. They were well expressed by our own philosopher John Locke in 1690 when he wrote in his Essay on Civil Government: " Whoever has the legislative or supreme power of any commonwealth, is bound to govern by established standing laws, promulgated and known to the people, and not by extemporary decrees; and by independent and upright judges, who are to decide controversies by those laws."

THE INSTINCT FOR LIBERTY

The second instinct of which I spoke, the instinct for liberty, finds its expression in certain fundamental principles of law. In order that free will, and not force, should be the basis of government, there are three fundamental requisites which must be fulfilled: (1) there must

---

[3] *Jacobs* v. *London County Council* [1950] A.C. at p. 373.

be freedom of discussion so that the people may criticise the existing government and propose an alternative; (2) there must be freedom of association so that people may form themselves into a party to advocate an alternative government; (3) there must be free and timely elections so that the people may have the government they choose. But experience has shown that these freedoms can only be secured by the rule of law; and can only be granted to those who propose and advocate a government which will recognise these self-same freedoms in others.

FREEDOM OF DISCUSSION

The keystone of our political liberty is freedom of discussion. In former days people used to think that our liberty was secured by the sovereignty of Parliament, but that has become a thing of the past. Over one hundred years ago Parliament was no doubt the supreme power in the land, both in law and in fact. The House of Commons was elected by a selected class of the people— the householders—and the House of Lords was an hereditary body which could veto any Bill except a Money Bill. Members of the House of Commons were unpaid and were expected to vote according to their conscience and not according to the dictates of a party. All that has altered now. The House of Commons is elected by everyone over the age of 21 and the House of Lords can no longer veto any Bill, it can only suspend it for a year. Members of the House of Commons are paid £1,000 a year and are not as independent as they were. Nearly all legislation is initiated by the executive and members of the government party are expected to endorse it. This was strikingly shown in a recent debate in the House of Lords where experienced parliamentarians stated the present situation in these words: Lord Simon said, " there is undoubtedly a greatly increased practice of regarding the individual, to whatever Party he may belong, as being an automaton who, if he attends, will obey the call, and will, therefore, from time to time authorise the Cabinet to do what the Cabinet wants, whatever it is ": Lord Cecil said that " If they show any disposition to take an independent line, information is conveyed to them that they will not be the Party candidates at the next Election "; and Lord Salisbury said, " private Members during recent years have been driven more and more into the Party Lobby, irrespective of their personal views." [4]

I am not concerned with whether this is desirable or not. It may very well be necessary in the interests of efficiency. All I would point out is that, if it is correct, it means that in practice sovereignty no longer rests with Parliament. It rests with the executive and in particular with the Cabinet. The Ministers of course gain their authority by being leading members of the party which wins the general election. So it may be said that ultimately they are dependent on the will of the majority of the people. But this is a very remote control, not only because there may be a general election only once every five years, but also because it is often impossible to ascertain what the will of the majority is upon any particular topic.

THE DOCTRINE OF THE MANDATE

The remoteness of this control has given rise to many misgivings lately. Take for instance the doctrine of the mandate. Before a general election the rival parties issue manifestoes giving details of all that they propose to do if they are elected. Once elected, the leaders claim that they have a mandate to carry out everything which

[4] *Hansard* for May 17, 1950.

was in their manifesto.   Nothing of course could be further from the truth.   Many of the people do not study these manifestoes in detail.   Those who do often find in each of them much of which they approve and much of which they also disapprove.   But they cannot pick out the bits of which they approve and vote for those bits only.   They have to vote for a member, not for a manifesto.   The personal qualities of the member do not weigh so much in the scale nowadays as they used to do.   This is no doubt because his personal views do not count so much in the House of Commons as they used to do.   Much more important are the views of the party to which he belongs and to which he has to conform. Hence the importance of its manifesto.   Some people vote for him because they approve of some of the proposals in his party's manifesto, others because they approve of others of the proposals.   Yet others because, while they do not really approve of the proposals, they disapprove still more of the counter-proposals of the rival party, and so forth.   It is impossible to say therefore that the majority of the people approve of any particular proposal, let alone of every proposal in the manifesto. Yet that is what the doctrine of the mandate involves. It is, I venture to think, a complete misconception of the constitutional position to suppose that the party which is elected has a mandate to carry out their manifesto or is, so to speak, under a trust to carry out all they have proposed.   If there were any trust in the matter, the courts could inquire whether it has been fulfilled, which is unthinkable.   The true constitutional position is that no radical change, that is, no change which is so radical that the views of the electorate should be obtained on it, should be made unless the proposal has been included in the manifesto; but that is very different from saying that everything that is in the manifesto should be carried out.

Once elected the leaders of the party are the sovereign power in the land. The only limitation on them is that they are under a constitutional duty to govern in the interests of all and not in the interests of party. They must therefore discard their manifesto, if and in so far as the course of events, or subsequent reconsideration, shows it not to be in the interests of the country as a whole. But this is not a duty which can be enforced by law. The only real check on their power is the force of public opinion.

CRITICISM OF THE GOVERNMENT

This brings me back to the importance of the freedom of discussion. Public opinion cannot be instructed, nor indeed can it be ascertained, unless there is freedom of discussion; and freedom of discussion involves, of course, freedom to criticise the government. Now experience has shown that governments are very sensitive to criticism. The reason is of course because governments realise that they are ultimately dependent for their power on the support of public opinion; and if the confidence of the people in them is destroyed by justifiable criticism, their position is rendered insecure and their chances of winning the next general election are lessened. They can of course object to unjustifiable criticism, but who is to judge whether the criticism is justifiable or not? History shows many cases where governments have considered any criticism of themselves as unjustifiable. In the seventeenth and eighteenth centuries many people were tried in England for seditious libel when all they had done was to criticise the government. In Nazi Germany and Soviet Russia any criticism of the party in power was regarded as treason. The truth is that, if there is to be political liberty, the government which is criticised must not be allowed to be the judge of whether the criticism is justifiable or not. The people themselves must judge: and they can only do so if there is freedom of discussion, so that they can have before them both the criticism and the answer to it.

Herein lies the great importance of Parliament at the present day. It still remains the forum where the opposition can level criticism at the government and where the government can make their reply to it. It still remains the place where questions may be put to the ministers on matters of public concern, which they must answer or take the consequences in public mistrust. There are, I fear, some notable exceptions, as for instance questions as to the day-to-day administration of the nationalised undertakings—but, taken by and large, the government have to answer in Parliament for their conduct of public affairs. Next to Parliament comes the Press, which is free to criticise the government and to ventilate grievances of all kinds. Its importance is realised by ministers who continually hold press conferences so as to instruct public opinion; and at these conferences the journalists themselves ask questions so as to gain further information. Then there is the British Broadcasting Corporation, which gives times for broadcasts not only to government spokesmen but also to speakers of other parties. It is essential to political liberty that all these powerful means of influencing opinion should be free to put all relevant facts before the public and to give voice to the views of all, whether for or against the government of the day.

FREEDOM OF THE PRESS

It is of course possible for this freedom to be abused. Anxieties were recently aroused lest the Press should become the monopoly of a few private owners who distorted the news and gave a false picture so as to serve their own ends; but the recent Royal Commission reported that " the present degree of concentration of ownership is not so great as to prejudice the free expression of opinion or the accurate presentation of news or to be contrary to the best interests of the public." Even greater anxieties would be aroused if the State took control of the Press, because it would then be able to prevent criticism of itself, which is the keystone of our liberties; but it is reassuring that the Royal Commission said that " nearly everyone would agree that State control ought not to be extended to the Press."

The greatest danger at present lies in the fact that the Government Departments are the source of much news and information; and they are naturally inclined to present it in a favourable light from their own point of view, or to withhold it if it is unfavourable; and so the Press may not have the information on which to base legitimate criticism. The Royal Commission uttered a warning about this. They said that " if newspapers get out of the habit of giving their own news and into the habit of taking all or most of it unquestionably from a Government Department, they are obviously in some danger of falling into totalitarian paths. Future developments therefore need to be carefully watched." [5] This vigilance is a healthy sign that the spirit of our constitution is still making itself felt so as to see that our liberties are not taken away.

CRITICISMS BY THE JUDGES

The sources of criticism of which I have already spoken are all frankly partisan and known to be so. In Parliament discussion runs on party lines. So it does in the Press and in broadcasts, and nowadays also in municipal

[5] Royal Commission on the Press, 1949: paras. 543, 617, 672.

elections. Indeed, many sources of criticism are to be discounted by reason of party bias. But there is one source which is not so to be discounted. It is criticism by the judges. Observations by them may form an important basis of public opinion. This carries with it the responsibility of being wise and discreet in all they say, but it does not mean that they must say nothing. If matters come before them where injustice is being done, they are entitled to point it out so that the public may know of it and form an opinion upon it.

Two or three years ago, however, an attorney-general laid down in the House of Commons a limitation on the judges. He declared that it was " a most important principle of our constitutional practice that judges do not comment on the policy of Parliament, but administer the law, good or bad, as they find it. It is [he said] a traditional doctrine on which the independence of the judiciary rests." [6] The fact that an Attorney-General said that does not mean that it is correct: but I do not think that anyone would quarrel with it so long as it is not carried too far. The judges, of course, administer the law, good or bad, as they find it. A good deal of it is made by Parliament, and so they must act in accordance with what Parliament says. They should show proper respect for, and confidence in, what Parliament has decided and should always carry out faithfully the intentions of Parliament. If a judge or magistrate should say, " I do not agree with this statute or regulation, and therefore I will only inflict a nominal penalty," he would be doing a grievous wrong. Nor should a judge enter into any captious or irresponsible criticism of what Parliament has done. If a judge should say to a young blackguard, " I wish I could have you birched, but Parliament in its wisdom says I cannot," that borders

[6] *Hansard*, May 3, 1950,

on the captious, or at any rate displays a want of confidence in Parliament which it is undesirable to express. But Parliament is not infallible. Its policies may have results it did not foresee. Its enactments may not work out in practice in the way in which it had intended. The draftsmanship may be obscure and give rise to unexpected difficulties. When this happens, the judges have the right and indeed the duty to point it out: and in the past they have often done so without being accused of impropriety. The judges are able to see how the Acts of Parliament work in practice and, when defects appear in them, their observations may be a great help to those responsible for making or amending the law. Not only the public but also the legislature may be left in ignorance of the defects unless they are pointed out to them.

The true principle, as I understand it, is that judges are entitled to make responsible comments or suggestions on the way in which Acts work, if it appears to them necessary to do so in the public interest. This applies not only in respect of enactments in ancient times but also in respect of enactments in modern times, subject to the qualification that judges must never comment in disparaging terms on the policy of Parliament, for that would be to cast reflections on the wisdom of Parliament and would be inconsistent with the confidence and respect which should subsist between Parliament and the judges. Just as members of Parliament must not cast reflections on judges so judges must not cast reflections on the conduct of Parliament. If everyone observes these rules, there will be no conflict.

THE PREACHING OF COMMUNISM

The result of it all is therefore that freedom of discussion is still an integral part of the British constitution. There is one qualification, however, that must be made about it. It must not be allowed to be abused so as to be itself undermined. This has been brought home to us by the preaching of communism. In England we allow the communists to advocate communism. We allow communist newspapers to be published, and before a recent general election a communist was allowed time on the wireless to broadcast in support of the communist candidates. This is a very healthy sign because it shows that freedom of discussion still prevails here. But we are told that, in Soviet Russia, where communism is practised, there is no freedom of discussion: and that, if anyone there says anything which is critical of the party in power, he is considered to be a danger and is to be imprisoned or otherwise dealt with. If this were the ultimate aim of the advocates of communism here, then it might well be said that the preaching of it should not be allowed: for it is taking advantage of the freedom of discussion so as to destroy that freedom. So also with other communist activities. They should not be allowed if the ultimate aim is the destruction of our fundamental freedoms. This is, no doubt, the justification for the strong measures taken against communists in various countries of the free world. The appropriate steps must always depend on the local situation. All I would say is that only extreme danger would justify any restriction on the freedom of discussion. A war of ideologies is not to be won by throwing people behind bars, but by " having your loins girt about with truth."

THE PRACTICAL INSTINCT

This brings me to the third instinct, the practical instinct to see that neither rights nor powers are exceeded or abused. This instinct runs through the whole of our search for justice and liberty. The English distrust abstract philosophy as much as they distrust formal logic. Some may suggest that this is because they do not understand philosophy or logic, but the better reason is because they know that they are apt to lead to error. The English approach is empirical. The solution to every problem depends on the question, Will it work? that is to say, Will it help to ensure justice and liberty? They take those conceptions as well understood and busy themselves with the machinery to enforce them. So they evolved the writ of habeas corpus, the great merit of which is that it is an efficient machine for liberating anyone who is unlawfully detained, and so also they have recently evolved the Crown Proceedings Act, 1947, which will, I venture to think, prove an efficient machine for seeing that Government Departments do not overstep the mark. Likewise the Scrutinising Committee for keeping a check on delegated legislation. This practical instinct finds its most marked expression in a readiness to compromise. Time and time again, when faced with two apparently irreconcilable alternatives, the English find a middle way. Thus when in time of war it was necessary to give to the executive power to detain suspected persons without trial, many people feared that our fundamental liberties were being infringed, but a compromise solution was adopted. A committee was set up, presided over by a distinguished lawyer, to examine every case so as to ensure that no injustice was done. It was really a fusion of executive and judicial functions to meet an emergency: and it worked well. So also in time of peace when it is necessary to give much new jurisdiction to departmental tribunals, many people fear that the rule of law is being ousted: but a compromise solution is being adopted. An appeal is gradually being allowed to an appellate tribunal presided over by a lawyer who is independent of the executive.

THE UNWRITTEN CONSTITUTION

It is this practical instinct also which leads us to believe in an unwritten as against a written constitution. The rigidity of a written constitution has its advantages for some peoples but it appears to us as an attempt by one generation to fetter the hands of future generations. The flexibility of an unwritten constitution has the great advantage that it enables us to make changes gradually, as and when they are needed, without a great deal of fuss and bother. It allows scope for compromise and room for development. Thus the power of the House of Lords has been gradually reduced from a power of veto to a power of suspension, and from suspension for two years to suspension for one year. A movement is on foot to reform the House of Lords altogether by altering its composition. All this is done by ordinary legislative machinery without anyone suggesting that the constitution is being infringed. We draw no legal distinction between constitutional laws and other laws. We can change a fundamental law just as easily as a transient law. But in point of practice we do not do so. We may modify our laws to meet changing needs, but we keep the fundamental principles intact.

THE FUNDAMENTAL PRINCIPLES

The fundamental principles are accepted by all parties in the State, and the only difference that can arise is as to application to particular circumstances. The principles were well stated by Viscount Jowitt, in the House of Lords when he was Lord Chancellor : " It behoves all of us who have been nurtured and brought up in traditions of liberty to see that those ancient privileges are not snatched away from us. . . . I quite agree, as I have said many times, that there is a danger today of the individual being crushed, and it is a danger against which we have to guard. What are the true remedies that we must follow? First of all, I believe we must have a vigilant, a resolute and strong Parliament. . . . Secondly, I believe that we must maintain a strong and independent judiciary . . . absolutely independent of any control at all. I thank God that I believe we have that today, and I think we shall always have it." [7]

There needs I think to be added the freedom of the Press; but this was added by Mr. Morrison when he was Lord President of the Council. After observing that the Labour Government could not expect a good Press from Conservative newspapers, he added, " We have, thank goodness, a Press free from the slightest improper inter-ference by Government authority, and it is my fervent wish that this should always be so."

A people, whose leaders speak thus, need have no fear for their liberties. So long as Parliament is vigilant, the Press is free, and the judges are independent, there can be no totalitarian State in England. Those three great institutions, Parliament, the Press and the Judges, are safeguards of justice and liberty: and they embody the spirit of the constitution which has made its impress on the character of the people.

This spirit of which I have spoken has been carried by our cousins to the great lands overseas, and it shines as brightly there as here. The colonies have become dominions and the dominions have become nations. Of them it can be said as truly as Sydney Smith said of the English nation over 130 years ago: " . . . Nations do do not fall which are treated as we are treated, but they rise as we have risen, and they shine as we have shone, and die as we have died, too much used to justice, and too

[7] *Hansard* for June 27, 1950.

much used to freedom, to care for that life which is not just and free. . . . [The] attributes of justice do not end with arranging your conflicting rights, and mine; they give strength to the English people, duration to the English name; they turn the animal courage of this people into moral and religious courage, and present to the lowest of mankind plain reasons and strong motives why they should resist aggression from without, and bind themselves a living rampart round the land of their birth." [9]

[9] *The Judge that Smites Contrary to the Law* (1824)

THE RULE OF LAW IN THE WELFARE STATE

WHAT are we doing to maintain the Rule of Law in the new social order which is called the Welfare State? I hope to show you that there has been a legal revolution equal in importance to the social revolution. There have been changes, many of them scarcely perceptible at the time, which have maintained the rule of law in our beloved land.

PUBLIC LAW BEFORE 1939

Let me start by reminding you of the state of our public law up to the outbreak of war in 1939. It was still governed by the theory that the central government of the country was carried on by the King himself with the assistance of his Ministers and other servants and agents. It was a maxim of the law that "The King could do no wrong." This was extended to mean that the Government Departments could do no wrong. If an army driver drove his 100-ton tank so negligently that he ran into the side of a house doing damage to the extent of £100, the householder could not sue the War Office for damages. The War Office was regarded in law as the Crown. It could do no wrong. The householder could therefore only sue the driver of the tank. It was just bad luck for the householder that the driver had not even 100 pence with which to pay the bill. The law ignored the fact that the War Office had put the overpowering vehicle into the driver's control.

It was another maxim of the law that the King could not be sued in his own courts. This was extended to mean that the Government Departments could not be sued in the Royal Courts of Justice. If the Ministry of Works

20

employed a builder to do work and they did not pay, he could not sue the Minister in the courts for the price. All he could do was to submit a humble petition to the King and then the Attorney-General, if he thought fit, could endorse it with the fiat " Let right be done." His right to payment depended therefore on the discretion of the Attorney-General.

In point of fact the position was not as bad as it sounds from my description of it, because in practice the Government Departments did not take advantage of the immunity which the law afforded them. If an army driver was ordered to pay damages for negligence, the War Office always used to foot the bill. If a Government contractor was not paid for his work, the Attorney-General invariably granted his fiat. Nevertheless you can see how dangerous this immunity might be if the central government came to be controlled by people with totalitarian ideas. The Government Departments could assert their great powers without any possibility of being challenged in the courts. They would, indeed, be above the law.

THE GOVERNMENT DEPARTMENTS

In view of this danger, it is important to record that one of the first things done by the Welfare State was to put the Government Departments under the law. It was done by the Crown Proceedings Act, 1947, but the story of how that Act came to be passed shows that the judges had a great deal to do with it. In 1921 Lord Birkenhead appointed a Committee to consider the position of the Crown as litigant. This Committee did not get on very fast. Three years elapsed and they produced nothing. Then in 1924 Lord Haldane became Lord Chancellor. He promptly told the Committee not to

waste time in talking. He relieved them of their duty
to make recommendations " as to whether it was desirable or feasible " to alter the law. He knew it was both
desirable and feasible. He told them to draft a Bill, for
that was all that was wanted. They did start on it, but
a few months later the Government fell, and Lord
Haldane ceased to be Lord Chancellor. Without him to
prod them on, the Committee again went leisurely. It
was three more years before they produced the draft
Bill. I must say that, when they did produce it in 1927,
it was a very good piece of work. But the Government
Departments put it on one side. They were anxious, no
doubt, to retain their immunities intact. They said
that no change was necessary. They claimed that any
injustice was avoided by the practice under which they
paid any damages awarded against any drivers or others
who did wrong.

THE ACTION OF THE COURTS

So the matter rested for nearly 20 years. The Government Departments retained their immunities and they
would, I suspect, retain them still today but for the
strong line taken by Viscount Simon when presiding
over the House of Lords in their judicial capacity. A
case [1] arose where military authorities had laid a minefield on some sand-dunes. They put a wire fence round
it but did not keep the fence secure. It was nearly
buried by sand in places. Some boys playing near it
kicked a tennis ball over the fence and ran to get it.
One boy was killed and another injured. The injured
boy claimed damages and the Treasury Solicitor put
forward an army officer as a nominal defendant. The
officer had in truth no responsibility for the minefield,

---

[1] *Adams* v. *Naylor* [1946] A.C. 543.

but the Treasury Solicitor said that he would not raise any defence on that ground and would let the case be decided on the merits. That would seem fair enough, but it was in truth a way of retaining the legal immunity of the Crown. It meant that the Treasury Solicitor would pay the damages as a matter of grace whilst asserting that in law the Crown could not be sued. Viscount Simon refused to allow this subterfuge. He said this : " The courts before whom such a case as this comes have to decide it as between the parties before them and have nothing to do with the fact that the Crown stands behind the defendant. For the plaintiffs to succeed, they must prove that *the defendant himself owed a duty of care* to the plaintiffs and has failed in that duty." I expect that Viscount Simon foresaw what would happen as a result of what he said. It meant that many a plaintiff, who had been injured by the negligence of Government Departments, was denied a remedy. A typical case came before the Court of Appeal [2] a few weeks after the judgment of the House of Lords. A woman employed in an ordnance factory was walking along a road inside the factory premises when she fell into a trench which had been recently dug and which was neither lighted nor fenced. The Ministry of Supply again put forward a nominal defendant. They named as defendant a man who had nothing to do with the accident, he was not the occupier of the factory, and had not been guilty of any negligence or breach of duty. He was clearly not liable at all. The Treasury Solicitor tried to overcome this difficulty by saying that, if there was any negligence by the Government Department, he would pay any damages which were awarded. But the Court of Appeal refused to let him do this. They refused to go into the merits.

[2] *Royster* v. *Cavey* [1947] K.B. 204.

The nominal defendant was himself under no liability. So they followed the advice of Viscount Simon and dismissed the claim.

THE CROWN PROCEEDINGS ACT, 1947

The courts thus exposed the glaring injustice of the Crown's claim to immunity. It meant that a person, who had been seriously injured by the fault of a Government Department, could recover no compensation. No civilised community could tolerate long such a state of affairs: and I suspect that that is what Viscount Simon and his colleagues foresaw. The only remedy for the injustice was to make the Government Departments responsible before the courts just as any other corporation or individual is responsible. There was, already in the pigeon-hole, as the House of Lords knew, the draft Bill which Lord Haldane had requested 20 years before. Lord Simonds, who was sitting with Viscount Simon, had himself been a member of the Committee which drafted it. He said that " no one who has experience of these matters will doubt that legislation on the subject of proceedings against the Crown is long overdue." The Bill was taken out of the pigeon-hole, touched up a little here and there, and passed into law as the Crown Proceedings Act, 1947. Only 14 months had passed since the judgment of the House of Lords in the case of the minefield—a short time for such a momentous achievement. It has placed the Government Departments fairly and squarely under the law. They appear now every day in the courts just as any other litigant.

THE SUBMARINE " THETIS "

Let me give you just one example of how beneficial this Act is. Most of you will remember, I expect, the case [3]

---

[3] *Woods* v. *Duncan* [1946] A.C. 401.

of the submarine " Thetis " which sank during her trials and 99 men died. Only four got out. Some of the builder's men were amongst those lost and their relatives sought to recover compensation. There was clearly negligence on the part of someone which caused the disaster but the relatives of the dead men were held by the House of Lords not entitled to recover from anyone. Someone on board had been negligent. The relatives tried to pin the blame on two of the naval men but did not succeed. There must have been some other naval man negligent whom they could not identify. If the law at that time had permitted the Admiralty to be sued for the negligence of any one of the naval men, there is no doubt that the Admiralty would have been held liable. But that could not be done. Viscount Simon had the difficulty in mind when he said: " If it be thought remarkable that after so long and elaborate an investigation no one should have been found liable for this loss of life, the answer is that in order to recover damages it is necessary to prove liability against one or other of the parties sued. The key to what is uncertain may have been lost among the ninety and nine who perished in the disaster." Nowadays, since the 1947 Act, the relatives could sue the Admiralty direct and could recover damages without having to prove which particular naval man was negligent.

THE NATIONALISED INDUSTRIES

So much for the Government Departments. They have been long with us. Let us now turn to the great bodies which have sprung, fully armed, from the womb of the Welfare State. I refer to the nationalised industries. Between 1946 and 1949, Coal, Railways, Gas, air transport, and many other undertakings were nationalised. The State owns them. The State appoints the Chairman and officers who run them. The Minister gives the general directions which they have to obey, but he leaves them to do their day-to-day business on their own. They are outside the control of Parliament, or at any rate, outside any close control. If these gigantic undertakings were to be above the law, it would indeed be a serious matter. If they were even to be regarded as agents of the Government Departments, it would be almost as bad because the Government Departments still have considerable privileges and immunities. But the judges have made it quite clear that they are as much subject to the law as any private individual.

The matter first came up for decision in regard to house property. You will know of course that nearly all the dwelling-houses in this land are controlled by the Rent Restriction Acts. The rents are pegged at the 1939 level and the landlords cannot evict the tenants except in very rare circumstances. Now the Government Departments are not bound by those Acts, because Parliament did not say they were to be bound. That seems at first sight a little strange but it is perhaps understandable when you think of married quarters or houses owned by the Admiralty or the War Office to accommodate their men. They may on occasions need them for the defence of the realm and it would not be for the good of the country that any impediment should be put in the way. But if that exemption were extended to the nationalised industries it would be a very different thing. The colliery companies and the railways for instance used to own a large number of cottages which they let out to their workers and to others. If the effect of nationalisation were that the tenants were thereafter not protected by the Acts, it would mean that their rents could be raised without limit and they could be ejected on a week's notice. The issue was taken to the courts and it was held that the nationalised industries were bound by the Rent Restriction Acts just like a private landlord.

THE BRITISH TRANSPORT COMMISSION

It is an interesting sidelight on our way of doing things that this important constitutional question was decided in a case [4] between two private individuals. A railway company had let a house to a tenant who had in turn sublet it to another. Upon nationalisation the head-tenant claimed that the house became Crown property and exempt from the Acts so that he could eject the sub-tenant. In this case, arising as it did between head-tenant and sub-tenant, the court held that the house did not become Crown property. The court laid down the position of the British Transport Commission in these words " In the eye of the law, the corporation is its own master and is answerable as fully as any other person or corporation. It is not the Crown and has none of the immunities or privileges of the Crown. Its servants are not civil servants, and its property is not Crown property. It is as much bound by Acts of Parliament as any other subject of the King. It is, of course, a public authority and its purposes, no doubt, are public purposes, but it is not a Government Department nor do its powers fall within the province of Government."

That decision about the nationalised industries has been accepted without question in other cases. You may remember that a year or two ago the Yorkshire Electricity Board was prosecuted [5] because it had erected a large building for its headquarters staff without a proper licence under the Defence Regulations. Counsel for the prosecution in opening the case stated that " a nationalised industry is not above the law " and no one said him nay.

[4] *Tamlin* v. *Hannaford* [1950] 1 K.B. 18.
[5] *The Times* newspaper, November 17, 1951.

It was found guilty and fined £20,000 and ordered to pay
all the costs, whereas if it had been regarded as a servant
or agent of the Crown, it would have been exempt. You
may ask, What good does it do to fine a nationalised
undertaking when the money to pay the fine has to come
out of the pockets of the public who own the undertaking?
The answer is that it does a great deal of good in that it
teaches those who run these undertakings that they are
subject to the law. It must be remembered that members
of Parliament are not allowed to ask questions about the
day to day administration of these undertakings. It is
very necessary therefore that it should be open to question
in the courts of law.

THE DANGERS OF MONOPOLY

One of the dangers of nationalisation is the monopoly
which it confers on the nationalised body. The law has
grasped this nettle firmly. It arose in a recent case
arising out of the nationalisation of the docks.[6] Some
tug owners—a family concern—had provided tug services
at Grimsby for over 60 years. After nationalisation the
Docks Executive sought to exclude these tug owners from
providing tug services for the Immingham Dock. The
reason was because the tugs belonging to the private
owners were fully employed whereas the tugs belonging
to the Docks Executive were idle. No one wished to
employ them. They could not hold their own in a busy
port. The Docks Executive sought to eliminate the
private owners so as to benefit their own tugs. The
private owners complained to the court. The judge, Mr.
Justice Sellers, held that the Docks Executive had no
right to exclude the private owners and he added significantly: " So far as I understand the position, the

---

6 *Pigott* v. *Docks and Inland Waterways* [1953] 1 W.L.R. 94.

decision at which I have arrived is more likely to provide efficient and suitable towage services at this important port than if the defendants' claim for a monopoly had prevailed."

THE HOSPITALS

The hospitals, however, afford the most striking illustration of how a nationalised undertaking has been brought under the rule of law. In the days before nationalisation, the law was very tender towards the charitable hospitals. It realised that they were dependent on voluntary contributions and that patients were treated gratuitously. The law did its best therefore to relieve them of liability. The leading case [7] arose over 40 years ago. A patient at St. Bartholomew's Hospital was severely burnt on the arm whilst undergoing an operation. A hot water bottle had been left touching him whilst he was unconscious. He claimed damages against the hospital authorities and failed. One of the Lords Justices said that the hospital authorities were not liable for the negligence of doctors or nurses in the course of their professional duties. This dictum was believed to be the law for over 30 years until the coming of the county council hospitals. In 1941 a radiographer on the staff of a county council hospital applied the X-rays too fiercely and burnt a child. The Court of Appeal held that the county council were liable for his negligence. [8] This opened the way to a reconsideration of the liability for doctors and nurses. It came to a head in 1951 after the hospitals had been taken over by the State. A man had gone into a hospital at Liverpool because two of his fingers were stiff and he wanted them made good. He came out with four stiff fingers and his hand was practically useless. It was

[7] *Hillyer* v. *St. Bartholomew's Hospital* [1909] 2 K.B. 820.
[8] *Gold* v. *Essex County Council* [1942] 2 K.B. 293.

clearly due to the negligence of somebody on the staff,
though nobody could say whose fault it was. The Court
of Appeal held that the hospital authorities were liable.[9]
In so doing they had to depart from the dictum of 40
years before; but they had no hesitation in doing it.
That decision has had widespread repercussions. Before
nationalisation a case against a hospital was a rare
thing. Now it is a very common thing. I do not
suppose there is more negligence than there was before.
The difference is that there is now a recognised legal
remedy against the nationalised service. Not every
point has however been cleared up. Only a few weeks
ago a hospital management committee sought to avoid
an action on a technical ground. The committee said
that they were protected by the National Health Service
Act from any liability for negligence but Mr. Justice
Parker rejected the contention.[10]

DEPARTMENTAL TRIBUNALS

Enough of nationalisation. Let us now turn to the
other phenomenon of the Welfare State—the growth of
departmental tribunals. In former times whenever Parliament created new rights and liabilities it almost invariably entrusted their determination to the ordinary
courts of law. Now it rarely does so. It sets up specialist
tribunals to deal with them. If these tribunals were to be
the mere tools of the Government Departments, it would
be the beginning of the end of the rule of law in this
country. There was at one time some danger of this.
The members of the tribunals are usually appointed by
the departments. They have often no real independence.
They are appointed for the particular case or for a

---

[9] *Cassidy* v. *Ministry of Health* [1951] 2 K.B. 343.
[10] *Bullard* v. *Croydon Hospital Management Committee* [1953] 2
W.L.R. 470.

specified period, and if they do not give satisfaction they are not appointed again. There is often no right of appeal from the tribunal to the ordinary courts. The departments can issue instructions by circulars telling the tribunals the principles on which they are to act. This made some people think that the departments were in control of the tribunals: and all the more so because it was thought that the ordinary courts had little power to interfere. It was thought that the courts had no power to interfere with a tribunal, no matter how wrong the tribunal might be, unless it had actually gone outside its jurisdiction.

THE NORTHUMBERLAND CASE

In 1951 a case came before the courts which altered the situation completely. It arose in this way: Upon the nationalisation of the hospitals, one Thomas Shaw lost his employment as clerk to the Northumberland Hospital Board. He was entitled by the regulations to compensation on a prescribed scale according to his length of service. The compensating authority granted him a sum which was too little. They had failed to credit him with many years service. He appealed to the Compensation Appeal Tribunal. The tribunal dismissed his appeal, although he was entitled to a larger sum. The tribunal had gone wrong in law. They had interpreted the regulations wrongly. The problem was, how could the matter be put right? The Attorney-General said it could not be put right at all. The decision of the tribunal, he said, was final: and no court could alter it. So long as that decision stood, the compensating authority dare not pay Mr. Shaw the money to which he was entitled, because, if they did so, the auditor would surcharge them. What was to be done? Recourse was had to one of the most ancient

writs known to the law, the writ of certiorari. This
writ is just as important to the rule of law as is the writ
of habeas corpus. Just as habeas corpus enables the
Queen's Bench to set free any man who is unlawfully
detained, so also certiorari enables the court to quash
the order of any tribunal which is given contrary to
law. The writ is a command directed to the tribunal
commanding them to send up the record of their proceedings for examination by the judges. So Mr. Shaw
applied for this writ. He applied to the Court of King's
Bench for a writ of certiorari to quash the decision of
the tribunal, and they did quash it. The Lord Chief
Justice, Lord Goddard, gave a convincing judgment
which was affirmed by the Court of Appeal. It was
held that the Court of King's Bench by the ancient
writ of certiorari has an inherent jurisdiction to control
all inferior tribunals : and that this control exists not
only to seeing that inferior tribunals keep within their
jurisdiction but also to seeing that they observe the
law. The result was that the decision of the Northumberland Compensation Tribunal was set aside and Mr.
Shaw got the compensation to which he was entitled.[11]

THE PROCEDURE TO CONTROL TRIBUNALS

The importance of that case cannot be over-stated.
It means that all the departmental tribunals are subject
to the rule of law: and when I say the law, I mean
the law as declared by Her Majesty's judges and not the
law as declared by the Government Departments. Take
for instance the compensation tribunals such as were in
question in the *Northumberland Case*. There are
numerous similar tribunals set up to assess the compensation payable to men who lose their employment owing

[11] *R.* v. *Northumberland Compensation Appeal Tribunal* [1952] 1
K.B. 338.

to nationalisation. Before the *Northumberland Case,* any one of these tribunals might interpret the regulations in a different way from another tribunal. No one would know which was right, and the department might feel it necessary to issue a circular giving its own views on the matter. Since the *Northumberland Case* if a tribunal is in doubt about a point of law, it can set out its reasons for the decision of the Court of Queen's Bench, which will then lay down the law for the guidance of all tribunals. So also with the rent tribunals which ascertain the proper rent payable by a tenant. Many difficulties were experienced because the various tribunals all over the country were deciding points of law differently. The Lord Chief Justice some little time ago suggested that there should be an appeal tribunal set up to resolve these points and keep the rent tribunals on the right lines, but the suggestion did not commend itself to the Government Department and it was not adopted.[12] Now the court itself has shown the way in which they can be kept within the law. The tribunal has only to set out the reasons for its decision and then the matter can be brought before the Court of Queen's Bench to see whether the reasons are right.

The one defect in that procedure by <u>certiorari</u> was that the point of law had to appear on the face of the proceedings, " on the face of the record " as it is said. <u>If the tribunal simply announce their decision without disclosing the point of law, that form of remedy is not available</u>. Even this defect has, however, been overcome to some extent. It arose in a dispute about the way in which lightermen should work in the Port of London. Some of the men had been suspended. A tribunal set up under statutory authority decided adversely

[12] *R.* v. *Brighton Rent Tribunal* [1950] 2 K.B. 410; *Hansard* for June 27, 1950.

to the men but did not set out its reasons. The dockers sought to say that their suspension was invalid. They could not proceed by certiorari because they had not enough knowledge to do so. So they brought an action for a declaration. It was held by the Court of Appeal that this procedure was open to them and the court declared that their suspension was invalid.[13]

STATUTORY COMMITTEES

So the process goes on. Gradually the courts are seeing that statutory tribunals obey the rule of law: and not only statutory tribunals, but statutory committees also. These too are a significant feature of the Welfare State. Committees are set up by statute to decide something or other in a judicial way but no appeal is given from their decision. Suppose they go wrong in law, can they be put right? The point arose for decision in connection with the new legal aid system, under which the State pays the legal costs of people who cannot afford to pay the costs themselves. A dealer in films claimed that some manufacturers had supplied him with defective materials and he brought an action against them claiming damages. He had not got enough money to pay his solicitor. So he applied for legal aid and was granted it, which means that the State would pay his costs. Before the action came for trial he was adjudicated bankrupt and a chartered accountant was appointed trustee in the bankruptcy. The chartered accountant wished to continue the action on behalf of the film dealer's creditors. The creditors ought thenceforward to have paid the cost of the action, but, instead of insisting on the creditors paying, the chartered accountant applied for legal aid and the committee

[13] *Barnard* v. *National Dock Labour Board* [1953] 2 W.L.R. 995.

granted it to him, which meant that the State would pay the costs. When the matter was investigated, it became quite clear that the legal aid committee had in law no power to grant the chartered accountant any legal aid: but nevertheless it was contended by the Law Society and by the committee that no one had any power to correct their decision. Lord Goddard pointed out what this meant. He said, " The Act is to help poor persons to take proceedings; the use of public funds to enable trustees in bankruptcy to bring actions for the benefit of creditors, who may be very wealthy concerns, seems quite foreign to its intention: but that will be the position if this court cannot intervene." The court did intervene. In an important judgment prepared by Mr. Justice Parker, it quashed the legal aid certificate which the chartered accountant had obtained: and thereby showed that these new statutory committees are not allowed to be a law unto themselves.[14] This decision went further than any case had done before. The Court of Queen's Bench has always claimed the right to control inferior courts but it has been very cautious in exercising control over administrative bodies. It will not seek to control them in regard to questions of policy but it will interfere when they go wrong in law on a matter which it is their duty to decide according to law.

PRIVATE TRIBUNALS

So far I have spoken of statutory tribunals and statutory committees, but there is another set of tribunals which are just as great a danger to the rule of law. I refer to the tribunals set up by the trade unions and other trade organisations to determine the rights of their members. These tribunals are not set up by statute but by the rules

[14] *R.* v. *Manchester Legal Aid Committee* [1952] 2 Q.B. 413.

of the organisation concerned. They wield powers as great as, if not greater than, any exercised by the courts of law. They can deprive a man of his livelihood. They can ban him from the trade in which he has spent his life and which is the only trade he knows. What if they dismiss him contrary to the justice of the case? Can the courts intervene? It has always been recognised that the court can intervene if the tribunal goes fundamentally wrong in matters of procedure, for instance, if it condemns a man without giving him notice of the charge against him, or without giving him an opportunity of being heard. But until quite recently it was thought that the courts could not intervene simply because the tribunal had decided contrary to law. The courts have now held that they can intervene. One illustration will suffice to show how important it is that the court should have this power. A cornporter in charge of a gang in the London Docks was charged with breaking one of the rules about unloading ships. It was not a serious breach, and he honestly believed himself to be innocent. But the men's committee found him guilty and ordered him to pay £6. He was so upset that, after the hearing by the committee, in the street outside, he struck the trade union official who had convened the committee meeting. He hit him in the face. It was only a minor assault for which he could have been taken before a magistrate who would probably have only fined him or bound him over to be of good behaviour in the future, and no more. But the trade union official did not take the man before the magistrate. He took him before the committee again. They removed his name from the Register of Cornporters and told the Port of London Authority not to employ him any more : and the Authority did as they were told. The man applied to the courts for redress and it was held

that the committee had acted unlawfully.[15] The man's
name was restored to the register. This case—and there
are others like it—show that the courts recognise that
" a man's right to work is just as important to him as,
if not more important than, his rights of property. The
courts intervene every day to protect the rights of
property. They must also intervene to protect the right
to work." [16]

KNOWLEDGE OF REGULATIONS

Much has been done therefore, to bring the Government
Departments, the nationalised industries and the
numerous tribunals under the rule of law. But there are
still some privileges and immunities attaching to the
Crown which are not altogether consonant with justice
to the individual. One of the difficulties inherent in the
Welfare State is the vast number of orders and regulations which are issued by the Government Departments.
The ordinary man is in theory expected to know all of
them. At any rate if he does something in breach of the
regulations, it is no answer for him to say that he did
not know there was such a regulation. That rule is
obviously necessary if the regulations are to have effect
at all. But suppose that an ordinary citizen, anxious to
keep within the law, inquires of an official whether there
is any regulation on the point and the official gives him
the wrong answer? It has been held that this affords
him no excuse. The ordinary citizen has no right to rely
on any statement by any official, however eminent. He
must seek out the regulation himself, though he will
be lucky if he knows where to find it, and having found
it, he must construe for himself what it means, though
often the best legal brains may differ upon it.

[15] *Abbott* v. *Sullivan* [1952] 1 Q.B. 189.
[16] *Lee* v. *Showmen's Guild* [1952] 2 Q.B. 329.

BUILDING REGULATIONS

Let me give some illustrations of the perils to which
citizens are subject. Under the Defence Regulations it
was unlawful for building work to be done unless it was
authorised by a licence granted by the appropriate
authority. Some building contractors were employed to
make alterations to some garages. They were granted a
written licence to do work up to £35. The licence was
signed by the licensing officer. While the work was being
done, it became clear that the work would cost a good
deal more than £35. So the building contractors saw the
licensing officer, and he told them, by word of mouth,
that they could go on and complete the work if it did not
exceed £100. On the faith of his assurance they did
complete the work, and they did it for less than the
£100, indeed for £70. The owner of the garages then
refused to pay the £70. He said that as the written
licence was only for £35, the rest of the work was illegal.
That defence, surprisingly enough, succeeded.[17] It was
quite clear that the owner had asked for the work to be
done and that it had all been done with the authority of
the licensing officer and that the proper charge for it was
£70. Yet because the written licence was only for £35,
the building contractors were held entitled only to £35.
The moral is that the building contractors ought not to
have relied on the word of the licensing officer. They
ought to have insisted on having it in writing. But how
were they to know it ought to be in writing, especially
when a distinguished lord justice (who dissented) thought
that word of mouth would suffice?

Perhaps we have not heard the last of this subject.
A recent decision of the House of Lords suggests that
there may be a way out of the difficulty. It arose in a

[17] *Jackson, Stansfield* v. *Butterworth* (1948) 64 T.L.R. 481.

ship-repairing case. The licensing officer there had
issued a written licence covering a good deal of the
contracted work, indeed it covered all the work required
to make the ship sea-worthy, but it did not cover the
installation of a cocktail bar. The licensing officer gave
permission for the cocktail bar by word of mouth only.
That was a technical defect and the owner of the vessel
sought to take advantage of it. He said that that defect
made all the work illegal—and so it did on the strict interpretation of the matter—and that he was not liable to pay
for it. But at the hearing the licensing officer came
forward and gave evidence that he had given permission
for all the work to be done, including the cocktail bar. The
House of Lords held that his evidence on oath made up
for the want of a proper written licence.[18] There was
admittedly a defect in the licence, but the House refused
to allow the owner to rely on it. " To do so," said
Lord Normand, " would be to stretch the precedents
beyond reason and to pass from reality into formalism
and make-believe." That decision was obviously just,
and it suggests that if you can get an official to come and
give evidence on your behalf, you can overcome the
difficulty of no written licence. So far, so good, but it is
not all officials who are so amenable !

" ESTOPPELS BIND THE CROWN "

Outside the licensing sphere, however, the courts have
not allowed the Government Departments to go back on
their word any more than a private individual is allowed
to do so. The Government Departments have on occasion sought to do so. It happens in this way. One
official tells the ordinary citizen one thing and he acts
on it, then another official comes along and says that the

[18] *Howell* v. *Falmouth Boat Construction Co.* [1951] A.C. 837.

first official was wrong. When the poor citizen exclaims
" But your people told me it was all right and that is
why I did what I did," the second official relies on Crown
privilege. He says, " I know that ordinary people
cannot go back on what they say—they are, to use
the lawyers' phrase, ' estopped ' from doing it—but
estoppels do not bind the Crown." I am glad to say
that that unjust doctrine has now been exploded. The
courts have not allowed it in the Welfare State. Let me
give two striking illustrations. An army officer who was
injured in an accident claimed that his disability was
attributable to war service. The War Office accepted the
view that it was so attributable and, on the faith of their
statement, he did not trouble to get a medical officer in
support of his case. Later on the Ministry of Pensions
tried to go back on what the War Office had said. They
sought to withhold his pension on the ground that his
injury was not attributable to war service. The court
refused to allow them to do this.[19] The officer got his
pension. More recently, after a house had been damaged
by enemy action, the War Damage Commission accepted
responsibility for paying the cost of making it good
amounting to £6,000, but later they sought to reduce
that sum by saying that the house was a total loss not
worth repairing and they would only pay the net value
of it, £1,600. Mr. Justice Vaisey held that, once the
Commission had unconditionally accepted liability for
the higher payment, they could not afterwards go back
on it.[20]

DISCOVERY AGAINST THE CROWN

There is one further privilege, however, which the
Government Departments have succeeded in retaining

[19] *Robertson* v. *Ministry of Pensions* [1949] 1 K.B. 227.
[20] *Re 56 Denton Road, Twickenham* [1953] 1 Ch. 51.

intact. It is the privilege of keeping their documents to themselves and not letting other people see them. No one except Government Departments can do this. Suppose you are involved in litigation and you have private documents which bear on the matter in dispute, you must produce them so that the court can see them, and also the other side. <u>Even if they hurt your case, you must produce them</u> so that the courts may be able to find out the truth and do justice. Not so, however, with the Government Departments. They are entitled to withhold any documents which the head of the department says it is contrary to the public interest for them to disclose. No one can object to this privilege so long as it is kept within reasonable bounds. No one for instance would wish the Royal Air Force to disclose documents concerned with aircraft still on the secret list. But the Government Departments are in this respect the judges in their own cause. If the head of the department says it is contrary to the public interest to disclose the documents, that is the end of the matter. The courts cannot inquire further. This privilege has sometimes been thought to be carried too far. A few months ago a man who was in prison at Winchester awaiting trial was assaulted by a mental defective in the same prison. He claimed that the officers of the prison had not taken proper steps to keep the mental defective under control and brought an action for damages against the Home Office. The Home Office refused to disclose the daily reports of the officers. The man lost his case, but Mr. Justice Devlin made some pertinent observations. He had, he said, " an uneasy feeling that justice may not have been done " because the material before him was not complete; and he added that Crown privilege was becoming a serious obstruction to the administration

of justice. If this is right, it means that the Government
Departments are inclined to see this thing too much from
their own angle. Their argument seems to be that, if
they should produce documents prepared by civil
servants, that will lead those servants to be too secretive.
In short, that they will not give full or frank reports for
fear that those reports may afterwards see the light of
day. It may be doubted whether this view does justice
to our fine civil service.

In consequence of what Mr. Justice Devlin said,
questions were asked in the House of Commons. The
Attorney-General was asked whether he would advise
the Government Departments to adopt a less rigid atti-
tude with regard to disclosure. But his reply was that
it would not be proper for him to give any such advice.
He said that the Ministers took great care to apply the
principles laid down by Lord Simon, the Lord Chancellor,
in the leading case [21] on the subject : " It is not enough,"
said Lord Simon, " that the Minister of the department
does not want to have the documents produced . . . he
ought not to take the responsibility of withholding pro-
duction except in cases where the public interest would
otherwise be damnified, for example, where disclosure
would be injurious to the national defence, or good
diplomatic relations, or where the practice of keeping a
class of documents secret is necessary for the proper
functioning of the public service." Those last words are
what the Government Departments seem to have sometimes fastened upon. They feel that it is necessary for
the proper functioning of the service to keep the documents secret. But there must be quite a temptation for
a Minister to persuade himself of this when he is
responsible for its proper functioning ! Let us hope that

[21] *Duncan* v. *Cammell Laird* [1942] A.C. 624.

he will resist this temptation whenever it stands in the path of justice.

THE OFFICE OF LORD CHANCELLOR

One last thing I would mention, and that is the changing conception of the office of Lord Chancellor. You will have noticed how often I have had occasion to quote from the speeches of Viscount Simon, made when he as Lord Chancellor presided over the deliberations of the House of Lords in their judicial capacity. During the five years in which he held that office, he regularly sat as the highest judge in the land and laid down principles of great importance in the law. In so doing he was carrying on a tradition which had lasted for many centuries. Lord Haldane advocated a change in this position. He said that if a Lord Chancellor was to be able to do his work properly, he could only do so if he were relieved of the daily duties of a judge who hears cases. That change has now come about. I think that in some ways it is a pity that it should have to be so, but it cannot be helped. And it is only right to say that many benefits have come from the change. The great lawyers who have held the office of Lord Chancellor in recent years have done much to preserve the Rule of Law in the land. Lord Jowitt's time as Lord Chancellor is marked by the Crown Proceedings Act, 1947, which put the Government Departments under the law, and by the Legal Aid Act, 1949, which has done away with the reproach that there is one law for the rich and another law for the poor. Lord Simonds' time has already been marked by notable steps which I need not mention now.

I have done. I have scampered across many fields. I have not dwelt upon the great political, social and economic changes effected in the last few years. They are obvious to all. I have been concerned only to show how the common law has adjusted itself to meet these changes. It looked at one time as if the Rule of Law itself would be washed away as by an unprecedented tide. But the gaps are being closed and the walls rebuilt. The Rule of Law is being maintained in the Welfare State.

THE CHANGING CIVIL LAW

LAWYERS are taught, from their youth up, that judges do not make or alter the law, but only expound it. The judges themselves have fostered this belief. If they are invited to amend or extend existing rules, they often say " We are not here to legislate " as if that were itself an answer to the invitation. The truth is that they do every day make law, though it is almost heresy to say so. I wish to take you through some of the changes which have been made in recent years, without the intervention of Parliament, in those parts of the law which were considered well settled.

LANDLORD AND TENANT

In the days before the wars, the law of landlord and tenant had reached a high degree of certainty. The judges had defined with precision the difference between a tenant and a licensee—it depended on possession. They had divided tenancies into set categories which seemed to exhaust all possibilities, tenant at sufferance, tenant at will, tenant from year to year, tenant for years, and so forth. They had laid down strict rules about the requisites of notices to quit. They had made rules about assignment and forfeiture. All was settled—settled on the philosophy of *laissez-faire*—the philosophy which leaves everyone to look after himself to his own best advantage. The landlord was at liberty to demand the highest rent which he could extort. He was entitled to eject the tenant in accordance with the strict letter of the contract: and to turn him into the street even though the tenant had nowhere else to go. The landlord was not bound to repair the house unless he expressly covenanted to do so and that he rarely did. He could allow the house to become quite unfit to live in for aught the law cared. Yes, the law was settled; settled in favour of the landlord.

The present century has witnessed a reversal of the position. Parliament has intervened time after time to redress the balance in favour of the tenant. It has intervened on the philosophy of the Welfare State—the philosophy which says that the State should look after those who are unable to look after themselves. Parliament started it in the first Housing Act by putting the landlord under an obligation to repair the houses which he let to the poor. He was made to keep them in a state reasonably fit for human habitation. Afterwards, under the pressure of war conditions, Parliament intervened drastically with freedom of contract. Houses were in short supply and the demand for accommodation was great. People would pay almost any rent to get a roof over their heads. So Parliament enacted the famous—or infamous—Rent Restriction Acts which prevented private landlords from raising the rents of dwelling-houses and also from evicting the sitting tenants. This was followed by Acts protecting the shop-keepers and farmers so that they should not be turned out of their holdings without compensation when they had built up a good business there. More recently still, recognising the importance of feeding the people, Parliament has taken agricultural land in large measure out of the realm of contract and out of the hands of the courts and has entrusted its administration to departmental officers and departmental tribunals. All these great changes are to be found in the Statute-book. I will not detain you with the tedious task of going through the statutes. They do not settle the law with any certainty. The broad principles underlying the statutes are clear enough, but the detailed application of them gives much work for the lawyers. What I want to do is to show you the remarkable influence which these statutes have had upon the old common law of landlord and tenant.

THE RENT RESTRICTION ACTS

In order to understand what I have to say, you must first realise that the Rent Restriction Acts protect a tenant who is living in his own home. He is protected for life so long as he cares to live there himself: and after he dies, his widow or (if he leaves no widow) his son or daughter can stay on there for life if they were living with him before he died. The family can stay with complete security of tenure for two lives and the rent cannot be raised. It is pegged at the 1939 level—and in some small dwellings at the 1914 level. The only thing that is necessary to confer these great benefits on a tenant is that he should have gone into the premises originally as a tenant, or have been accepted by the landlord as a tenant. Once he is a tenant, he is protected. Another significant thing is that the parties cannot contract out of the Acts. Even if a tenant agrees to pay a higher rent, he can throw over that agreement the next day and stay on at the standard rent for life. If he pays more than the permitted amount, he can recover back the over-payments.

THE EXEMPTION OF LICENSEES

Now comes the point. The benefits of the Rent Restriction Acts are conferred only on tenants, not on licensees. Landlords have therefore sought in many cases to say that the occupier was not a tenant but only a licensee. In the days before the war nearly everyone, who was in exclusive possession of a house and paid rent for it, was regarded as a tenant and not as a licensee. But since the war there have been many cases where a person in exclusive possession has been held to be only a licensee.

The first case was decided only two years ago. A family had lived in a house protected by the Rent Acts for many years. The father lived his life there and died. His widow stayed on until she died also. His daughter then wanted to stay on also, but the landlord was reluctant to let her become a tenant. He was not bound to accept her as a tenant, because the two lives permitted by the statute—the father and the mother's lives—had expired. The landlord was therefore entitled to turn the daughter into the street. He did not want to do that: but the difficulty was that if he accepted the daughter as tenant, it would mean that the statute would start running afresh for two more lives, that is, for the life of the daughter herself and after her death for a member of her family. In order to get over the difficulty, the landlord told the daughter that she could stay on at the old rent for a few months so as to give her a chance of finding other accommodation; but he refused to give her a rent book, because he did not want to create a tenancy. He allowed her to stay for six months, accepting rent from her, but when he sought possession she claimed to be a tenant protected by the Rent Acts. Now under the old law it is very probable that on payment and acceptance of the weekly rent, the daughter would have been held to become a weekly tenant. In those days it would not matter much whether she was a tenant or a licensee, because if she was a tenant she could be turned out on a week's notice. In these days it makes all the difference. If she was a tenant she could stay for life and her own child after her. If she was a licensee she had no right to stay against the landlord's wishes. The Court of Appeal held that the daughter was only a licensee: the Master of the Rolls pointed out how wrong it would be if the landlord, in order to preserve his rights, were compelled to turn the daughter out immediately her mother died. The landlord ought not to be penalised by doing the generous thing of allowing her to stay for a while until she could find somewhere to go. So the daughter was held to be a licensee only.[1]

That case was followed by many others. I will go to the latest of them. A company had business premises with a flat above which had a separate entrance but also had direct access to the business portion. They let the flat to the managing director on a tenancy for some years but he then left their employ and went to work for some-one else. He asked the company if he could stay on in the flat at the same rent for a time so that he could look for other accommodation, and he made it clear that he did not seek to stay as a controlled tenant protected by the Rent Acts. The company thereupon allowed him to stay on and accepted rent from him. Later when they sought possession he set up the Acts. He said that he was a protected tenant and could stay for the rest of his life. Mr. Justice McNair held that he was not a tenant but only a licensee and he had to go.[2]

Now these cases, you may say, come very near to allowing people to contract out of the Rent Acts—a thing which is forbidden by Parliament. The law says, however, that it is not contracting out. It is the creation by the parties of a different relationship—a licence and not a tenancy—which is not caught by the Acts.

THE STATUTE OF LIMITATIONS

The importance of the distinction will be realised when I tell you that it has been applied, not only in cases about

[1] *Marcroft Wagons, Ltd.* v. *Smith* [1951] 2 K.B. 496.
[2] *Murray Bull* v. *Murray* [1953] 1 Q.B. 211.

the Rent Acts, but also in cases about the Statute of Limitations. Under the law in force 50 years ago it was held that if a man allowed his gamekeeper to live in a cottage for 13 years without paying rent, the gamekeeper became the owner of the cottage and was entitled to it absolutely.[3] The basis of that decision was that the gamekeeper was a tenant at will who was deemed, after his first year, to become a squatter, and then by staying on another 12 years he gained a squatter's title. At the present day the law would not do anything so unjust. The gamekeeper would be held to be a licensee, and not a tenant at will, and not therefore entitled to rely on the Statute of Limitations.[4]

In all this legal history is only reflecting itself. Some centuries ago when the law originally created the " tenancy at sufferance," it was for the very purpose of preventing the true owner's entry being defeated by a squatter. So today when the law has created the residential licensee, it is for the very purpose of preventing the true owner's entry being defeated by the Rent Restriction Acts or the Statute of Limitations contrary to the justice of the case.

I will not seek today to define with precision the difference between a tenancy and a licence. That can only be done when enough cases have been decided out of which to formulate the principles. That is no drawback. It is our way of doing things. We do not seek, as Continental jurists do, to lay down principles first by abstract reasoning and then apply them to concrete cases. We decide the cases according to their merits and then see what principle emerges from them.

---

[3] *Lynes* v. *Snaith* [1899] 1 Q.B. 486.
[4] *Cobb* v. *Lane* [1952] 1 T.L.R. 1037.

CONTRACTUAL LICENCES

There is one more change in the law of land which I must mention though it has nothing to do with the Rent Acts. It is the matter of <u>contractual licences</u>, by which I mean contracts by an owner of land or premises to allow another to come on to them and use them in some way or other. Instances are the contract made when you take a <u>seat for a theatre</u>, the contract when a householder agrees to let a business firm put up an advertisement sign on his house, the contract when a theatre-owner agrees to let caterers have the use of the refreshment rooms, and so forth. None of those are tenancies. They are only contractual licences. At one time the law treated these contracts in a most extraordinary fashion. It was said that the owner of the premises was entitled to revoke the licence at any time. Thus in the cases I have mentioned, he was entitled to turn out the theatre-goer, tear down the advertisement sign, or eject the caterers as he pleased, and the law was powerless to stop him. It could not intervene by way of injunction against the owner. The only redress of the injured person was an action for damages for breach of contract which might be a quite inadequate remedy. Another extraordinary thing was that if the owner chose to sell his premises to someone else, the purchaser could disregard the contractual licence altogether. It was not binding on him and he could revoke it without being liable in damages at all.

Five years ago the House of Lords pointed the way to a change. Lord Simon and Lord Uthwatt both said that, since the fusion of law and equity, the courts could and would intervene by <u>injunction</u> to prevent the owner of the premises from revoking the licence in breach of the contract.[5] Once this is established, the next

[5] *Winter Garden Theatre* v. *Millenium* [1948] A.C. 173, 191, 202.

question which arises is this: If the owner sells his premises to another who takes them knowing that the owner has already granted a licence to an advertiser to put up a sign or to a caterer to use refreshment rooms, can the purchaser of the premises revoke the licence at any time he pleases? Is he not in the same position as the previous owner from whom he bought? It would seem strange if the purchaser could disregard the licence. If he could the original owner would have a simple way of avoiding his obligations. All he would have to do would be to form himself into a company, sell the premises to the company, and let the company revoke the licence.

If the purchaser is bound, it means that a contractual licence is an equitable interest in land. This would be a matter of great significance but it would not be so revolutionary as some people might think. Over 100 years ago the courts of equity enforced contractual licences when they had been acted upon by the execution of works on the land. A typical case was when a father by word of mouth promised to give his son a plot of land, knowing that his son intended to build on it. The son built a house on it but the father never before his death conveyed the land to the son. It was held that the son was entitled to compel the father's representatives to convey the land to him.[6] The only difference between the old cases and the new ones is that in the old cases the licensee expended money on works on the land whereas in the new ones he expends time and energy in doing things on the land. That is not a difference in principle but only in the application of it. In both cases you will find that the contractual licence is specifically enforceable against the owner and his successors, if, but

[6] *Dillwyn* v. *Llewelyn* (1862) 4 De G.F. & J. 517.

only if, it has been acted on by entry and presence on the land.

To conclude this review of changes in land law, you should notice that the contractual licences of which I have first spoken have much in common with the residential licences which I mentioned earlier. They are both governed by the same principles and look very like a new form of tenure of land, but they are not so. The essential feature of each licence is that it is not a right of property. It is a personal right or privilege, personal to the licensee which he cannot assign or sublet. But it is enforceable against purchasers who take with notice. It is therefore an equitable interest.

THE LAW OF CONTRACT

Turning now to the law of contract, the most remarkable change has been in the doctrine of consideration—the doctrine which holds that, in order that a contract should be binding, some benefit must be given or some detriment suffered by the party who seeks to enforce it. The doctrine of consideration has existed in the law for 350 years. It survived a strong onslaught by Lord Mansfield and a weak thrust by Lord Blackburn. It treated with contemptuous silence the recommendation of Lord Wright and his colleagues on the Law Revision Committee. Yet it has crumbled under the advancing tide of the new equity.

PAYMENT OF A SMALLER SUM

The most conspicuous injustice perpetrated by the doctrine of consideration was the rule that payment of a smaller sum is no consideration for the discharge of a larger sum—a rule which was given apparent permanence by a decision of the House of Lords in 1884.[7] The

[7] *Foakes* v. *Beer* (1884) 9 App.Cas. 605.

injustice of the rule was brought into the full light of day during the war when many a creditor agreed to accept part payment of the sum owing from the debtor and to waive any claim to the balance. According to the doctrine of consideration the part payment was no consideration; the waiver was not binding on the creditor, and he was entitled to sue for the balance which he had deliberately forgone. Most creditors, let it be said in fairness to them, did not seek to take advantage of this unjust rule of law. Nearly all those who agreed to waive their debts stood by their waiver. The only question with which the courts have had to deal is the extent of the waiver. Thus in one case where a landlord of a block of flats agreed to forgo part of his rent whilst the flats were empty, the only question was at what date could he revert back to the full rent.[8] In another case, when the owner of a patent agreed to forgo part of his royalties during war conditions, the principal question was what notice had to be given before he could charge the full royalty.[9] If the waiver by the creditor was not binding on him at all, he could have insisted on full payment despite his waiver; but in each case the courts held that he was bound by his promise to forgo, and that the extent of the waiver depended on the true scope of the promise. In the case about the royalties, the Court of Appeal said that the creditor ought to give nine months' notice before he could again insist on the full royalties. In coming to those decisions, the courts expressly applied a doctrine of equity which says a court of equity will not allow a person to enforce his strict legal rights when it would be inequitable to allow him to do so.

[8] *Central London Properties* v. *Hightrees House* [1947] K.B. 130.
[9] *Tungsten Electrical Co.* v. *Tool Metal Co.* (1950) 69 R.P.C. 108.

DOCTRINE OF EQUITY

This doctrine warrants the proposition that the courts will not allow a person to go back on a promise which was intended to be binding, intended to be acted on, and has in fact been acted on. By turning the light of this new equity on to the old common law we can give at once the true reason why a composition with creditors is binding. It is because each creditor has made a promise to accept a reduced amount and the debtor has acted on the promise. We also see why, on the retirement of a partner, an agreement by a creditor to accept the liability of the continuing partners and to release the retiring partners is binding on him. It is because the retiring partners have acted on the promise. So many of the old cases can be explained by the new doctrine which were inexplicable by the doctrine of consideration.

VARIATION OF A CONTRACT

Another injustice, also sanctioned by a decision of the House of Lords, was the rule that the variation of a contract, in order to be binding, must be made for good consideration; and if the original contract needed to be in writing, the variation must be in writing too.[10] This injustice had rankled for some years before the war but was brought to a head by the many cases after the war when sellers—makers of goods—were unable to give delivery at the contract date. The buyers were so anxious to get delivery that they said that they would extend the time and accept the goods so long as they were delivered within, say, three months. On the faith of that assurance the sellers would go on and complete the goods and offer them within the three months. Could the buyers then turn round and refuse to accept

[10] *Morris* v. *Baron* [1918] A.C. 1.

them? There was no consideration for the variation by which the buyers agreed to accept them, and it was often not in writing. Nevertheless the courts have held that the buyer was liable for non-acceptance.[11] In another case a buyer was bound under the contract to open a letter of credit forthwith in favour of the seller. Afterwards the seller promised to let the buyer know when the goods were ready and said that the buyer need not open the letter of credit until he was notified that the goods were ready. On the faith of the promise, the buyer did not open the credit. There was no consideration for the promise and it was not in writing. Nevertheless the seller was not allowed to go back on it.[12] He could not complain that the credit had not been opened when he himself had not fulfilled his own promise. He had given no notice that the goods were ready. In these cases again the courts applied the same broad principle of equity which I have already mentioned that a person will not be allowed to go back on a deliberate promise which has been acted upon.

REPRESENTATIONS OF FUTURE CONDUCT

The third injustice which was at one time authorised by the House of Lords was the rule laid down in 1854 that estoppel applies only to statements of fact and not to representations as to future conduct.[13] According to this rule a representation as to the future had to be embodied in a contract or it was nugatory. The injustice of this rule was so apparent that the House of Lords in 1877 themselves unconsciously departed from it. It arose in a case where a landlord gave a

[11] *Rickards* v. *Oppenheim* [1950] 1 K.B. 616.
[12] *Plasticmoda Societa* v. *Davidsons* [1952] 1 Lloyd's Rep. 527.
[13] *Jordan* v. *Money* (1854) 5 H.L.C. 185.

tenant six months' notice to repair. A little later he
entered into negotiations with the tenant to purchase the
lease. That amounted to a representation that he did not
intend to enforce the doing of the dilapidations pending
the negotiations. When the negotiations broke down, he
sought to insist on the original six months' notice : but
the House of Lords refused to allow him to do so.[14]
They held that the notice did not begin to run until the
end of the negotiations. The landlord had made a representation as to his future conduct, from which he was
not allowed to withdraw. The interesting thing is that
the House of Lords did not themselves appreciate that
in this later case they were departing from their own
previous doctrine. They made no reference to it. The
result was that for many years the bad old doctrine was
repeated in the cases and was stated in the textbooks.
The later case remained hidden and forgotten, until it
was rediscovered in recent times and made the basis of
a new development which has taken the law of contract
by storm and has out-dated three leading cases in the
House of Lords. Shortly stated the effect of this new
development is that the doctrine of consideration does not
apply to the modification or discharge of contracts. If
one party, by words or conduct, promises to modify or
discharge the obligations of the other, intending that he
should act on the promise and he does act on it, then
the modification or discharge is binding, even though
there is no consideration to support it.[15] Thus the
doctrine of consideration has come to be limited to what
Sir Frederick Pollock said was its proper scope, namely,
to govern the formation of contracts.

[14] *Hughes* v. *Metro. Ry.* (1877) 2 App.Cas. 439.
[15] *Combe* v. *Combe* [1951] 2 K.B. 215.

ACTS DONE ON REQUEST

Turning now to the formation of contracts, the doctrine
of consideration, whilst still an essential requisite, has
been interpreted on much broader lines. It has long
been settled that an act done on request is sufficient
consideration to support a promise but this proposition
was often limited in its application. Professor Ames
contended that it should be extended to any act done on
the faith of the promise, and his view has now been
accepted. Stated in modern form the proposition is that
<u>a promise is binding if it was intended to be binding,
intended to be acted upon, and has in fact been acted
on.</u> Professor Gower has shown that it is only by this
proposition that all the various cases can be explained.[16]
Where a bank notifies a seller that it has opened a
confirmed documentary credit in his favour, and the
seller acts upon it by depositing the documents with the
bank, he is entitled to sue upon it. The bank has, of
course, already made a contract with the buyer to honour
the credit and the buyer has provided consideration for
that contract. But the issue of the credit in favour of
the seller is a different contract. It is a contract by the
bank with the seller for which there is no consideration
except the fact that the seller has acted upon it. When
an auctioneer announces that a sale will be made without
reserve, and a member of the public acts upon the
announcement by going to the sale and making a bid,
(and no one bids higher) the auctioneer is bound as soon
as the bid is made. He cannot withdraw the lot at that
stage or refuse to knock down the hammer. It is said
that the person making the bid has a right to withdraw it
at any time before the hammer has fallen. That is true,
and it means that there is no contract of purchase until

[16] 68 L.Q.R. 457.

the hammer falls. But there is another contract already in existence, whereby the sale is promised to be without reserve. That is a different contract for which there is no consideration except the fact that the bidder has acted upon it. When a dealer promises a customer that a car is in good condition, and on the faith of that promise the customer takes it on hire-purchase terms from a finance company, which exclude any condition or warranty, the customer can hold the dealer bound by his promise, although there is no consideration for it except the fact that the customer acted on it. In all those three classes of cases some one or other would have said formerly there was no consideration. <u>But the law is now settled that the very acting on the promise is itself consideration.</u>

This principle explains also older cases which were formerly inexplicable on the strict doctrine of consideration. If an uncle promises to pay his nephew £100 if the nephew marries the lady to whom he is engaged, some might say that there was no consideration for the promise because the nephew only did that which he was legally bound to do: but under this new principle as soon as the nephew married the lady the promise to pay £100 would be binding <u>because it was acted upon</u>. This principle opens up the way to a solution of the vexed question of whether the granting of a firm option for a fixed time is binding. At the moment some people think that a nominal consideration, such as 2s. 6d., must be given to make it binding; and that is still necessary if the option-holder does not act on it. But once he has acted on the faith of the promise, then the logical consequence of the modern cases is that the option cannot be revoked.

THE ONE SINGLE PRINCIPLE

Now I want you to combine the principles which relate to the formation of the contract with those relating to its

modification or discharge. It may ultimately be found
that common to both there is one single principle—that
a promise is binding if it is intended to be binding,
intended to be acted on and is in fact acted on. By
virtue of this principle all the injustices created by the
strict doctrine of consideration can be done away with,
and a simple test put in its place which meets the needs of
today and explains much that was inexplicable before.

THE DOCTRINE OF MISTAKE

Next to the doctrine of consideration, the most remarkable change has been in the doctrine of mistake. It
shows well how substantive law grows out of the remedies
available. The courts of common law had no power to
set aside a contract on the ground of mistake. All they
could do was to say the contract was a nullity, null and
void from the beginning. They had no other way of
granting relief. This meant that they were placed in an
awkward dilemma. The contract was either bad altogether or good altogether. If it was good, the court was
declining to give relief to an innocent party who had
entered into a contract under a mistake. If it was bad,
the court gave him relief, but often at the expense of
innocent third parties. For instance, in one leading case,
where the House of Lords held that a sale of goods was
void for mistake, it meant that an innocent third party
who had bought the goods in good faith had to give them
up or pay their value.[17] The infusion of equity has
removed that awkward dilemma. The court is now able
to set aside a contract on such terms as may be just.
The effect of this new remedy means that a contract will
rarely be held to be a nullity from the beginning. The
court will review the whole transaction and determine the

[17] *Cundy* v. *Lindsay* (1878) 3 App.Cas. 459.

rights of the parties as practical justice seems to demand. A good illustration is given by a case that arose under the Rent Acts. To explain it, you must understand that the Act prevents a landlord from obtaining more than the 1939 rent except when structural improvements have been made, and he is then allowed to make an appropriate increase on giving a formal notice. Now it so happened that a landlord agreed to let a flat to a tenant for 7 years at a rent of £250 a year. That was a fair and proper rent because improvements had been made which justified it. But unfortunately no formal notice of increase had been given with the result that the rent legally permissible was only £140 a year. The tenant soon afterwards discovered the mistake and said that he was only legally chargeable with £140 a year. He claimed to hold the lease for the full term of seven years at the low rent of £140 a year with all the advantages of assignability and so forth which are inherent in a lease but not in a statutory tenancy. In answer to the tenant's contention, the landlord sought to set aside the lease on the ground of mistake. Under the law of mistake as previously understood, the courts could only have done one of two things: either hold the lease to be a nullity from the beginning which would be unfair to the tenant because he would have to quit, or else hold it to be a valid lease for the full term at the low rent which would be unfair to the landlord. In the result the court took a middle course. It set aside the lease on terms which were fair to both parties. It allowed the landlord to put himself in order by serving a proper notice of increase and then making £250 the legally permissible rent; and, that being done, it gave the tenant the right to take a new lease at that rent which was only that which he had originally agreed to do.[18] This case undoubtedly heralds

[18] *Solle* v. *Butcher* [1950] 1 K.B. 671.

a new approach to the whole law of mistake. You have only to compare the most recent edition of the standard textbook of *Cheshire and Fifoot on Contract* with the previous edition to see that the chapter on mistake has been largely rewritten.

THE LAW OF RESTITUTION

Turning now to another subject, we find that the law of restitution is beginning to find recognition. It has had much to contend with. Enunciated by Lord Mansfield nearly 200 years ago, it was emphatically rejected by Lord Sumner and Lord Justice Scrutton, but has come back into favour under the guidance of Lord Wright. Let me tell you of some of the decided cases which show the way it is happening. The case of the Cairo sergeant takes first place. He was paid a large sum by some local Egyptians because he aided them in their illicit adventures. He used to sit on the front of a lorry in uniform and thus enable the lorry to pass through Cairo unmolested. The Crown claimed the money and took it from him. It was held that the Crown was entitled to it.[19] It can hardly be said that the sergeant contracted expressly or impliedly to pay the money to the Crown. Nor can it be said that it was recoverable as damages for breach of contract or for tort, because the Crown had in fact suffered no damage. If the sum was not recoverable in contract or in tort, on what basis was it recoverable? The House of Lords were content to decide the case on its own facts without saying into what category it fell. Lord Porter said guardedly that " the exact status of the law of unjust enrichment is not yet assured." Notice that he refers only to the law of unjust enrichment, not to the law of restitution. The law of restitution is, I think, assured. It comprises all those cases which cannot

[19] *Reading* v. *R.* [1951] A.C. 507.

be brought within the scope of contract or tort but in which nevertheless the plaintiff can recover money under the money counts or under some positive rule of law such as that applied in the Cairo case or even under the rules of equity as in the case of customers of the Birkbeck Bank.

Let me give another illustration from a decided case. A master employs a servant for 12 months by word of mouth. The servant serves his full time and sues for his wages. He cannot recover under the express contract because it was not in writing. He cannot recover under an implied contract because the express contract is still in existence. The effect of the Statute of Frauds is only to make it unenforceable; and you cannot have an implied contract covering the same ground as an express contract. But it is obviously just that he should be able to get the wages due to him: and there are cases, old and new, saying that he can recover them, or at any rate a reasonable remuneration equal to them. Seeing that he cannot recover on an express or implied contract, the only possible basis is in <u>Restitution</u> : and the Court of Appeal has recently so held.[20]

UNJUST ENRICHMENT

In truth, however, once you realise that there is a separate category of the common law—separate from contract and tort—which may be called Restitution, then cases almost tumble over one another to get into it. Take a case which arose the other day before Mr. Justice Harman. Two men went to an auction sale where a piece of land was for sale. Each wanted it to be kept as open land but they did not want to force the price up by bidding against one another. So they agreed together that one

---

[20] *James* v. *Kent* [1951] 1 K.B. 551.

I TLR 552

of them only should bid, but they did not come to any
definite arrangement as to what was to happen if the land
was knocked down to him. He did bid and did get the
land, and then he turned round and said it belonged to
him absolutely and he could do what he liked with it.
There was no contract between them because their
arrangements were so vague and uncertain, but nevertheless the judge would not permit the bidder unjustly to
enrich himself in that way. He ordered that the land
should be sold and the profit divided equally between the
two of them.[21] Likewise if a wrongdoer takes something
belonging to another man, for example a car, and then
makes use of it, he must pay a reasonable hire for it,
even though the owner has suffered no loss. It may be
that the owner would not have used the car himself,
or that he had a substitute readily available. Nevertheless the owner is entitled to a reasonable hire.[22] In
both these cases the judges seem to have proceeded on
the footing of unjust enrichment.

This new concept may enable us to solve many difficult problems. Take the case of an estate agent who is
employed on the usual terms, namely, that he is entitled
to his commission when the sale is completed and not
before. He introduces a purchaser who signs a contract
and pays a deposit of 10 per cent. of the price. The
purchaser then refuses to go on with the deal and his
deposit is forfeited. Is the vendor entitled to keep the
whole of the deposit without paying the agent anything?
The agent cannot make good a claim in contract because
the sale has not been completed. But he may perhaps
claim in restitution for the services he has rendered.[23]

21 *Pallant* v. *Morgan* [1953] 1 Ch. 43.
22 *Strand Electric Co.* v. *Brisford* [1952] 2 Q.B. 246.
23 *Boots* v. *Christopher* [1952] 1 K.B. 89.

Underlying all the law of restitution is the conception that no one should unjustly enrich himself at the expense of his neighbour. This conception is too indefinite to be stated as a principle of law: but it sufficiently indicates a new category. Just as the <u>conception of contract</u> is the enforcement of promises, and the <u>conception of tort</u> is damages for wrongdoing, so <u>the conception of restitution is the prevention of unjust enrichment</u>. Once this category comes to be accepted into the law, the courts will no longer find themselves forced to fit all remedies into the strait-jackets of contract and tort, but will be able to develop a comprehensive category with its own distinct principles.

THE LAW OF TORT

The law of tort has shown as great changes as the law of contract or restitution. The great majority of cases of tort coming before the courts are cases of personal injury. The law on them has been radically changed in recent years. <u>Whereas previously a plaintiff failed to recover anything if he was himself in part to blame, he now recovers reduced damages. Whereas a workman previously could not make his employer responsible for negligence of a fellow-servant, the employer is now liable for such negligence as if it were his own</u>. Previously when two persons were both liable for the injury to the plaintiff they could not recover contribution from one another, but now they can. I do not pause to describe these great changes in detail. They are due to Acts of Parliament which have proved very beneficial. I am only concerned in drawing your attention to the changes effected by the courts.

" LAST OPPORTUNITY "

First I mention the doctrine of last opportunity. Under it when two people are both guilty of negligence leading

up to an accident, it was held that the accident was
wholly due to the one who had the last opportunity of
avoiding it.   This doctrine gave rise to what Lord du
Parcq described as " a mass of verbal refinements, of
logic chopping, of the results of pointless microscopical
research."   The reason for the doctrine undoubtedly was
the rule of law that a plaintiff who was himself partly
to blame could recover nothing, even though the defendant was much more in fault than he was.   To avoid this
injustice, the courts held that the defendant was solely
to blame if he had the last opportunity of avoiding the
accident.   In 1945 the rule that a plaintiff could not
recover anything if he had been guilty of contributory
negligence was abolished by Act of Parliament.   With
the abolition of the rule, there was no reason to retain
the doctrine of last opportunity.   If the injury was the
result of the negligence of both, the damages can
be apportioned.   But the Act did not in terms abolish
the doctrine, and on a literal interpretation there was a
good deal to be said that the doctrine was not affected.
Nevertheless the courts have held that it no longer exists.
A typical case occurred recently when a lorry driver
negligently left his lorry diagonally across the road on
a foggy morning.   An oncoming motor-cyclist saw it but
negligently did not apply his brakes as promptly as he
should or take the appropriate avoiding action, and there
was a collision.   If the doctrine of last opportunity had
still been in existence, the motor-cyclist would have
recovered nothing, but both were held to blame and he
recovered damages, but reduced, because he was partly
at fault.[24]   A converse case occurred when a man, to get
a lift, carelessly stood on the tail-bar of a vehicle.   It
stopped for a moment and just then another motor-
vehicle came negligently round the corner and ran into

[24] *Harvey* v. *Road Haulage Executive* [1952] 1 Q.B. 120.

the man. If the doctrine of last opportunity still
existed, the injured man would have recovered in full
because, although he was negligent, the driver of the
oncoming vehicle was subsequently and severally negligent. The court held that both were to blame and he
only got reduced damages.[25]

WHO IS A SERVANT?

Another important change is the test of who is a servant.
A master is, of course, liable for any wrong done by his
servant in the course of his employment. It is often,
therefore, vital to decide whether the relationship of
master and servant exists. For a great many years it
was thought that it all depended on the right of control.
If a person had the right to give the man directions as
to the manner in which he should do his work, the relationship of master and servant was held to exist; but
otherwise not. This test had, however, long given rise to
misgivings because there are obvious cases where there is
no right in the employer to control the manner of the
work at all and yet the relationship is held to exist. A
good instance is the captain of a ship, or the pilot of an
aircraft. The employer has no right to give the orders
as to how they should carry out their duties but yet the
relationship exists. The matter came to a head in the
hospital cases. It had been said in 1910 that a hospital
authority was not liable for the negligence of their professional staff, nurses and doctors, because it could not
give them directions as to how they should treat the
patients: and this dictum was often followed in practice.
Very recently, however, that saying has been held to be
inapplicable under modern conditions. The relationship of
master and servant depends, not so much on submission

[25] *Jones* v. *Livox Quarries* [1952] 2 Q.B. 608.

to orders, as on whether the person concerned is part and parcel of the organisation. Nurses and doctors on the staff of a hospital are clearly part and parcel of the organisation, and on this footing the hospital authority is liable for them. This is a most important development, not only in hospital cases, but also in the general law of master and servant.

WHY IS THE MASTER LIABLE?

These hospital cases have, in a strange way, made the courts face the problem: What is the real reason why a master is made liable for the wrongdoing of his servant. It has often been assumed that the servant only is at fault, not the master: that the liability of the master is a vicarious liability which cannot be justified on any moral ground but only on grounds of expediency. In consequence it has been assumed that if the master is made to pay damages to some one who has been injured by the servant's negligence, he can call on the servant to indemnify him. On this footing the hospital authorities have recently sought to claim indemnity from doctors who have been negligent. They know that the doctors insure themselves against liability, so they claim an indemnity against the doctors, really meaning to get it from the insurers. When the claim for indemnity came to be discussed, no case could be found in which the indemnity had ever been given. A long time ago when witnesses were disqualified for interest, a court refused to let a servant give evidence for the master because the master might sue him for an indemnity. But there again the right to an indemnity was assumed. It was not decided. It was only last year that the courts were really faced with the problem. The answer to it is that the liability of the master is not truly vicarious. When the servant does an act in the course of his employment, that act is not only his own act but it is also the act of his master through him. The servant himself is no doubt under a duty to use reasonable care in doing it, but the master also is under a duty to see that it is done with reasonable care. If it is done negligently, the servant is a wrongdoer but so also is the master. They are joint wrongdoers. The master has not an absolute right to an indemnity. He is only entitled to such contribution from the servant as the court thinks fit to award him under the Joint Tortfeasors Act.[26]

This approach was strikingly confirmed by a case decided by the Lord Chief Justice where a wife and husband were both employed in a public-house. The wife was injured by the negligence of her husband while he was acting in the course of his employment. She could not sue her husband for damages because a wife cannot sue her husband for a tort and vice versa. But she was held entitled to sue his employer. That shows that the liability of the employer was not merely vicarious. He was not shouldering the liability of another. He was liable on his own account. The reason was because his servant's act was his act and he was answerable for the want of care in doing it.[27]

INVITEES AND LICENSEES

So far my discourse has been of progress. Now I must turn to places where the law has become " bound in shallows and in miseries." It is in the swamps inhabited by invitees and licensees. These creatures first saw the light in 1867 in the days before the spacious field of negligence was discovered. They were dissected and analysed

[26] *Jones* v. *Manchester Corporation* [1952] 2 Q.B. 870.
[27] *Broom* v. *Morgan* [1952] 2 All E.R. 1007; affirmed by C.A. [1953] 1 All E.R. 849.

in detail until the profession <u>thought</u> it knew the difference. <u>An invitee</u> was a person who came on to premises
on the owner's business or on a matter in which the owner
was interested. <u>To him the owner owed a duty to take</u>
<u>reasonable care not to injure him.</u> <u>A licensee</u> was a per-
son who came on to premises by the permission of the
owner but not on his business. <u>To him the only duty</u>
<u>owed by the owner was to use reasonable care to keep</u>
<u>the premises free from traps.</u> Two recent decisions of
the House of Lords have made the profession revise their
views on these subjects. The first was concerned with
the distinction between a licensee and an invitee. The
owners of a housing estate let a shop to a tradesman but
kept the forecourt in their own possession and control.
They negligently omitted to repair the forecourt and left
a stop-cock sticking up in a dangerous position. A customer who was going to the shop fell over the stop-cock
and was injured. Looking at the matter on principle, it
would seem fairly clear that she was an invitee. It was
obviously the business of the estate owners to keep the
forecourt in a good condition so as to make the approach
safe for customers. Their own financial interests
demanded that they should repair it: because if they did
not do so, the tradesman would complain and would be
unwilling to renew the tenancy or pay his rent. Apart
from their own financial interest, the plain fact is that
they were in control of the forecourt. If they were not
under a duty to the customer to repair it, no one was—a
proposition which is not at all creditable to the law. Yet
the House of Lords felt compelled by authority so to hold.
They held that the customer was only a licensee and not
entitled to recover because, although they were negligent,
the defect in the forecourt was not a concealed danger,
but an obvious one.[28]

[28] *Jacobs* v. *L. C. C.* [1950] A.C. 361.

The other case was concerned, not with the distinction between the two categories, but with the duty towards an invitee. A main contractor who was doing work on a ship erected a staging for the workmen to walk on. He did it in a very careless way so that it was dangerous and unsafe. He employed a sub-contractor for some work; and one of the sub-contractor's men fell from the staging and was injured. He had complained of it beforehand but the main contractor had taken no notice. There was therefore no doubt that the accident was due to the fault of the head contractor but nevertheless the House of Lords held that he was not liable.[29] The reason was because the man knew of the danger— indeed he had complained of it—and because he knew of it, he was disentitled to recover. This decision has surprised the profession. Lord Wright has said that the House, in reversing the Court of Appeal, has departed from the law as previously recognised: and you have only to look at the last edition of *Smith's Leading Cases* to see that is so. The most obvious comment upon the case is that it has reduced the difference between a licensee and an invitee to vanishing point. <u>The invitee is now disentitled to recover for known or obvious dangers which are not concealed.</u> So is a licensee. The invitee can recover for concealed dangers. So can a licensee. Another obvious comment is that whereas it is a general principle of law that a person cannot excuse himself for his negligence by saying that the injured person knew of it, nevertheless an invitor can do so. It is to be noticed that in that particular case the workman probably had a claim against his own employer, the sub-contractor, for not taking reasonable care to see that the staging was safe: but many invitees have no employer to look

[29] *Horton* v. *London Graving Dock* [1951] A.C. 737.

to, and it is in those cases that the decision may work injustice. Lord Reid, who dissented, observed significantly that " in the realm of negligence, at least, rigid rules give rise to what I believe is avoidable injustice."

Those cases show that the time has come when the law about invitees and licensees should be reformed : and it is all to the good that the Lord Chancellor has referred the subject to the Law Revision Committee. Some may hope that the distinction will be abolished and that the duty of an occupier will be made simply a duty to take reasonable care in respect of all those who lawfully come on to his premises whether at his invitation or by his permission, and whether on his business or not. It seems strange that a householder should owe a higher duty to a tradesman or canvasser who comes to solicit orders than he does to a guest whom he invites to dinner.

MODERN TRENDS

If you stand back and look at the development of tort from a distance, you will see that in the nineteenth century the judges were gradually making their way towards a comprehensive tort of negligence, but were introducing limitations lest it should get out of hand. They made distinctions between invitees and licensees, between things dangerous in themselves and those which were not dangerous, they refused to allow an action for negligent statements, they did not allow a manufacturer who issued goods under contract to be made liable in tort to a third person, and so forth. Some of those limitations have been swept away in the twentieth century, but several remain. The time has come for a complete clearance.

There is one more modern trend which I must notice.

For some time past many courts showed a marked tendency in accident cases to decide in favour of an injured workman and against the employer. The underlying assumption seems to have been that the risk should fall on the employer who benefited by the man's work and not on the injured man. The tendency has been checked by the extension of national insurance to which the employer and workman both contribute substantial sums each week. Inasmuch as the man now gets industrial benefit and medical treatment in any case, the courts have not been so inclined to decide against the defendant as once they did. In many cases lately it has been said that on a charge of negligence it is not sufficient to show that there was a foreseeable risk which might have been eliminated by the employer at great expense. It is always necessary to measure the risk against the measures necessary to eliminate it. Negligence should only be found if there is something that a reasonable man would do that the defendant did not do, or vice versa. This has always been the test in law but there was much room for variation in its application. Now that the risk of injury is largely borne by insurance, the right to compensation is made to depend more on blameworthiness than it did formerly. This is so, not only in cases between employer and workman, but also in accident cases generally. So does the law change in accordance with the needs of the times.

EQUITY

Turning now to equity, every student knows what equity is. It arises out of the tendency of all law to become rigid. It invokes the principles of natural justice. Equity claims that these principles have priority over all other laws, and can be prayed in aid to mitigate their harshness or soften their rigidity. In the days of Lord

Nottingham and Lord Hardwicke equity was very fluid
and adaptable : but in the hands of Lord Eldon it became
rigid and technical and it has remained so ever since.   A
new equity has arisen, as I have told you, to soften the
rigidity of the law of contract and the law of landlord
and tenant : but the old equity remains as rigid as ever.
Let me tell you of some cases which show this :

THE DIPLOCK CASE

The first, of course, is the case about Caleb Diplock's will.
Many years ago the equity judges, under the influence of
Lord Eldon, laid down the rule that if a man by will
left his property to trustees to distribute to " charitable
and benevolent purposes " it was a valid bequest, but if
he left it for " charitable or benevolent purposes " it was
bad ; and not only bad, but incurably bad.   This proved
to be a trap for at least two unwary solicitors and may
be for many more.   In 1939 a solicitor who had fallen
into the trap sought to blame it on to the typist.   He
said that, in drawing up the will, he dictated the word
" and " but the typist took it down as " or," and he
didn't notice it when he read it through, nor of course
did his unsuspecting client who knew nothing of the rules
of equity.   The President of the Probate Court, Lord
Merriman, was ready to help to extricate them from
the trap by striking out the word " or "; but the Court
of Appeal said that the Probate Court must not interfere
with the will.[30] /

This ruling came to the notice of a solicitor in Australia
who saw in it an opportunity for challenging the distribution of the Diplock money.   It arose in this way : the
solicitor who drew up the will of old Caleb Diplock had
fallen into the same trap, and the trustees had actually

---

[30] *Re Horrocks* [1939] P. 198.

distributed a quarter of a million pounds to charities which were both charitable *and* benevolent. But the will contained the deceptive word " or." It said that the trustees were to distribute the fund for " charitable *or* benevolent purposes." If the word " or " had been omitted, or had been " and," the bequest would have been good. But because the word " or " was there the House of Lords held that the bequest was incurably bad. No remedy was available by means of rectification or by severance or by any doctrine of *cy-près*. By this ruling the intention of the testator was utterly defeated. It was held that none of the money ought to have been paid to the charities at all. It ought to have gone to Caleb Diplock's first cousin once removed who was living in Australia and of whom he had never heard. No one can doubt that if Caleb Diplock or his solicitor had any idea that that might happen they would have struck out the word " or." [31] But that is not the end of the story. The first cousin once removed claimed the moneys back from the charities. Some of them had it still in the bank, so they of course had to pay it back. But others had spent it on building new hospital wards or repairing old ones or in paying their working staff, so they simply had not the money to pay back. On the faith of the bequest being valid, they had radically changed their position and, in point of natural justice, they would seem to have had a good equity to resist repayment. But nevertheless the House of Lords held that the charities personally must pay to the first cousin once removed every penny they had had. The decision was based on a ruling of Lord Nottingham 300 years ago when equity was still an infant. It was held that the first cousin once removed had an equitable right which was not to be denied. To anyone

---

[31] *Re Diplock* [1941] 1 Ch. 267 ; [1944] A.C. 341.

who is not a lawyer it must seem strange that equity should be invoked to do such injustice. It just shows how rigid equity has become.[32]

OTHER INSTANCES

Another recent case is *Armstrong* v. *Strain*,[33] where a man built a bungalow on shifting soil. He underpinned it several times but it remained very unsafe. He then put it into the hands of an estate agent for sale but told him nothing of the danger. The estate agent told a proposed purchaser that any building society would lend £1,200 on it because that represented a small percentage of the value. Thereupon the plaintiff bought the bungalow. A short time later the bungalow subsided beyond repair. Neither the owner nor his agent was guilty of fraud but they were between them guilty of an innocent misrepresentation. It was held that the buyer had no remedy. It is a rule of equity laid down over 100 years ago that, once a contract for sale of a house is completed by conveyance, there can be no rescission for innocent misrepresentation. This rule is so well established that in *Armstrong* v. *Strain* counsel for the plaintiff did not even claim rescission for innocent misrepresentation. Yet no one can doubt that as a matter of justice the buyer should have been allowed to rescind. Lord Justice Birkett said there was great force in the plea that the law should be able in some way to give the plaintiff redress, but there was none.

Instances could be multiplied of the failure of equity to adapt itself to modern needs. Take the case of a contract for the benefit of a third party. Nearly every other country in the world now gives the third party a

[32] *Ministry of Health* v. *Simpson* [1951] A.C. 251.
[33] [1952] 1 T.L.R. 82. Also [1952] 1 K.B. 232.

cause of action. But in England we are still bound by
the rule of law that no one but a party to a contract
can sue upon it. The injustice of this rule is seen by
what happened in *Miller's Agreement*.[34] A man sold his
business and in return the purchaser covenanted to pay
to the seller an annuity for his life and after his death
an annuity to his daughter for her life. The father died
and the daughter was held to have no right to sue for
her annuity. There can be little doubt that in the wise
and just hands of Lord Hardwicke the Court of Equity
would have found a remedy. Lord Hardwicke was ready
in all these cases to hold there was a trust in favour of
the third party and thus to give a remedy. The conception of a trust has, however, since his time been
narrowed and canalised so as to require as an essential
element a positive intention to create a trust.[35] By this
narrowness of outlook equity, to use Professor Hanbury's
phrase, is throwing away " the weapon it has itself
forged." Even section 56 of the Law of Property Act,
1925, which was wide enough in its terms to permit a
remedy, has been " construed in a very conservative
manner " and so the courts missed an opportunity of
modernising the law which the legislature offered them.[36]

REMEDIAL EFFORTS

Courageous efforts are now being made by some judges to
remedy the situation. Thus Mr. Justice Vaisey tried a
case recently where a man who had mortgaged his house
to a building society sold it to a purchaser. In the deed
of transfer the purchaser covenanted that he would pay
the future instalments to the building society. The building society was not a party to the deed of transfer, but

[34] [1947] Ch. 615.
[35] *Vandepitte's Case* [1933] A.C. 70.
[36] *White* v. *Bijou Mansions* [1937] Ch. 610, at p. 625.

Mr. Justice Vaisey held that the building society could enforce the covenant by direct action against the purchaser. He held that in this respect the deed of transfer was a deed poll; and that according to the old law a deed poll can be enforced by a person who is not a party to it. The decision is much to be welcomed but it would appear to be a recourse to an archaic distinction between a deed poll and a deed *inter partes*—so as to give a remedy which equity was powerless to give.[37] Similar bold action was taken by Mr. Justice Danckwerts in a case where a company was in possession of land and an option was given to the company to buy the freehold. The option was contained in an agreement made with the directors and not with the company; but nevertheless Mr. Justice Danckwerts held that the company was entitled to enforce it. He did this by praying in aid section 56 of the Law of Property Act, 1925.[38] Whether these two cases herald a new approach on this subject I do not know. They are too special in their nature and in their reasons to provide any clear guide to the future.

CONCLUSION

In telling you of all these changes, I have tried to show that the law is not static. It is developing continually. Those who emphasise the paramount importance of certainty in the law delude themselves. It is not certain and it is a mistake to think that it can be made certain.

[37] *Chelsea Building Society* v. *Armstrong* [1951] 1 Ch. 853.
[38] *Stromdale* v. *Burden* [1952] Ch. 223.

THE RIGHTS OF WOMEN

IN St. Matthew's Gospel you will remember the precept that " a man shall leave father and mother and shall cleave to his wife: and they twain shall be one flesh." [1] The common lawyers turned this into the principle that " by marriage the husband and wife are one person in law ": and the husband was that one. That principle has had a great influence on our law. Sir William Blackstone declared that " upon this principle of an union of person in husband and wife depend almost all the legal rights, duties and disabilities that either of them acquires by the marriage." [2] The scope of the principle was expressed by him thus: " The very being or legal existence of the woman is suspended during the marriage, or at least is incorporated and consolidated into that of the husband: under whose wing, protection and cover, she performs everything."

HER PERSONAL FREEDOM

That sounds very well: but the law took no notice of the converse precept that the husband was to love and cherish his wife. The magnanimous protector was authorised also to be a tyrant. Every husband was by law given power and dominion over his wife. It was said in the old books that he might keep her by force within the bounds of duty and might beat her, but not in a violent or cruel manner. The gloss put upon this by the common man was that he might beat her but only with a stick not thicker than his thumb. By

[1] Matthew xix, 5.
[2] Blackstone, *Commentaries*, I, 442.

the time that Blackstone wrote towards the end of the
eighteenth century this power began to be doubted
among the higher ranks of society: but he adds that
" the lower rank of the people, who were always fond
of the old common law, still claim and exert their antient
privilege; and the courts of law will still permit a husband to restrain a wife of her liberty in case of any gross
misbehaviour." [3] As late as 1840 when a wife threatened
to leave her husband, he was held to be entitled to keep
her a prisoner in the house and to use force for the
purpose. It was not until 1891 that the courts gave
her the right to come and go as she pleased. It was
decided in a celebrated case where the husband thought
he was well within the law.[4] His wife had left him and
he had obtained from the courts an order that she should
return to him. When she did not obey, he waited for
her one Sunday morning outside the church where she
had gone for the service. He had a solicitor's clerk with
him, and together they bundled her into a waiting
carriage and drove her off with her feet sticking out
of the door. They took her to the husband's house and
kept her there against her will. But one of her relatives
saw her at the window—just before the blind was hastily
drawn—and brought a habeas corpus. The court
ordered her release: and from that day to this it has
never been doubted that a husband has no right to
deprive his wife of her liberty.

The supposed right of a husband to beat his wife has
also disappeared. The reason it continued so long was,
I fancy, not because the law approved of husbands
beating wives, but because the law gave no effective
remedy. She could not sue him in the civil courts,
because he and she were one person in law: and it did

[3] Blackstone, *Commentaries*, I, 445.
[4] *R.* v. *Jackson* [1891] 1 Q.B. 671.

not do her any good to prosecute him in the criminal courts for assault and send him to prison. Since 1895, however, that has all been altered—she has an effective remedy before the magistrates. Nowadays if a husband strikes his wife, it is cruelty which may cost him dear. It does not take many blows to entitle the wife to a separation. He may find himself with no right to her services and liable to pay her maintenance for life. A few wives, I am afraid, have been known to abuse the position and to seek to provoke their husbands to strike them, so as to get maintenance without service. The courts are on their guard against devices of this sort. But at any rate the position now is that no husband can beat his wife with impunity.

HER DUTY TO OBEY

The result is, therefore, that a husband has no longer any power to coerce his wife into obedience: and, with the lack of any coercive power, he has lost his right to give her orders. Not long ago a husband found this out to his own cost. His wife would persist in going to see her sister. The husband objected and ordered her not to go. Yet she would go. So when she got back he hit her, and she had a nervous breakdown. She then brought a petition for divorce for cruelty. The judge who tried the case held that the husband had not been guilty of cruelty because she had only to obey him in order to be safe. But the Court of Appeal held that that was not the law. He had no right to give her such orders and they granted her a divorce.[5]

There was, however, until the last year or two one matter on which the husband could still dictate to his

---

[5] *Meacher* v. *Meacher* [1946] P. 216, but see *Jamieson* v. *Jamieson* [1952] A.C. 525.

wife. He could dictate where the matrimonial home was
to be. If she refused to live with him in the place he
chose, she was guilty of desertion, and liable to be
divorced. That was all very well in the old days when
husbands were always the wage-earners and the wives
stayed at home. He had to live near his work and had
the right to say where the home should be. But we
have got to a stage where wives often go out to work and
earn, maybe, as much if not more than the husbands.
The old rule has therefore disappeared, and has been
replaced by a rule which has been stated thus : " The
decision where the home should be is one which affects
both the parties and their children. It is their duty to
decide it, by agreement, by give and take, and not by
the imposition of the will of one over that of the other.
Each is entitled to an equal voice in the ordering of affairs
which are their common concern. Neither has a casting
vote, though to be sure they should so try to arrange their
affairs that they spend their time together as a family
and not apart. If such an arrangement is frustrated by
the unreasonableness of one or the other and this leads
to a separation between them, then the party who has
produced the separation by reason of his or her unreason-
able behaviour is guilty of desertion." [6]

PRESUMPTION OF COERCION

So long as the husband had power and dominion over his
wife, she did get one advantage out of it. If she stole
goods or committed any other felony in the presence of
her husband, the common law presumed that she had
done it under the coercion of her husband and she was
entitled to be acquitted. There is an interesting historical
explanation for this presumption. In the old days when

[6] *Dunn* v. *Dunn* [1949] P. 98.

husband and wife were charged jointly with a felony, the man, if he could read, was able to escape capital punishment by claiming benefit of clergy. In order to show that he could read, all he had to do was to repeat the first verse of Psalm 51: "Have mercy upon me, O Lord, according to Thy loving kindness : according to the multitude of thy tender mercies, blot out my transgressions." This he often managed to do, at any rate with the aid of a compassionate prompter. But women could not, in those days, be clergy any more than they can in our days : and so when the husband and wife were charged together, the wife, however well she could read, and however well she knew the psalms, had not the benefit of clergy, and was liable to be sentenced to death. The judges overcame this injustice by presuming that she committed the offence under the coercion of her husband : and this presumption remained in the law even after women were given benefit of clergy, as they were by Statute in 1692. It was not until 1925 that the presumption was abolished. Parliament then recognised that a husband no longer has coercive power over his wife. If she commits an offence in the presence of her husband, she is just as guilty as he is unless she proves that he did in fact coerce her into it.

The old law therefore whereby the husband was given power and dominion over his wife has completely disappeared. She is no longer a servant who is bound to obey, but a partner entitled to an equal voice in all matters of common concern.

TRACES OF SERVITUDE

Although equality has thus been achieved in principle, nevertheless there are still several traces to be found in the law of the wife's former servitude. The law used to treat her as if she was the chattel of her husband. If she was injured in a road accident by the negligence of the driver of a carriage, she could not by herself alone bring an action for damages. Her husband had to be joined as a plaintiff and, if damages were awarded for her pain and suffering, the husband could put them into his own pocket. That was not altered until 1882 when it was enacted that she could sue alone in her own name and any damages were to be her own separate property. But even today if the husband has lost the benefit of her services so that he has to employ extra help in the house, he can still recover damages for himself on that account. No one would, I imagine, doubt the justice of this, but it is really a survival of the time when the wife was regarded as a servant. The husband gets damages for the loss of his wife's services just as a master can get damages for the loss of the services of his servant. But the wife cannot get damages for loss of her husband's services. If her husband is so badly injured in an accident that he is rendered impotent so that the wife is deprived of the opportunity of having children, she cannot recover damages on that account.[7]

ENTICEMENT

In the old days, if anyone persuaded and enticed a wife to live separate from her husband without sufficient cause, the husband was entitled to bring an action for abduction and claim damages. The old law was so strict on this point that if a wife missed her way upon the road, it was not lawful for another man to take her into his house unless night was falling and she was in danger of being lost or drowned. The only thing apparently that a stranger might do was to carry her

[7] *Best* v. *Samuel Fox* [1952] A.C. 716.

behind him on horseback to market. The action for abduction still survives to this day, but it is known as an action for enticement. Some of you may remember the case where a doctor was said to have enticed away the wife of a grocer's assistant. The evidence turned a good deal on the doctor's words to the wife : " Come on, Gwen, we will go." He was found liable for enticement and ordered to pay heavy damages.[8] In the old days a wife could never bring an action for abduction of her husband : but in recent times—since the action has been put into modern dress as an action for enticement—it has been held that a wife can bring an action against another woman who entices away her husband. Actions of enticement are, however, rarely brought, and still more rarely do they succeed. If a husband is allured away by a designing woman, a jury is not inclined to give the wife any damages against the other woman. They attribute the situation more to the husband's folly than to the success of the temptress. Likewise if a wife is enticed away by an unscrupulous adventurer, a jury are often not inclined to give the husband much damages. They feel he should sue for divorce and not for enticement.

The truth is that in modern days actions for enticement are an anachronism—a relic of a past age—as also, some may think, are actions for breach of promise of marriage. These actions treat betrothals and marriages as if they were legal contracts subject to all the legal rules in regard to breaches of contract : whereas they are in truth solemn promises which are more a matter for the honour and conscience of the parties than a subject for money claims in a court of law.

[8] *Place* v. *Searle* [1932] 2 K.B. 497.

DAMAGES AGAINST CO-RESPONDENT

Somewhat similar to the action for enticement is a claim for damages against a co-respondent in a divorce suit. A wife whose husband has committed adultery cannot claim damages against the other woman, but a husband can claim damages against the man who commits adultery with his wife. This difference in treatment is again a survival from the time when the wife was regarded as her husband's chattel. The husband's action was originally in trespass—which is the same kind of action he would bring as if his horse had been lamed by the defendant. It was called an action for criminal conversation and in the old days the damages were usually large and exemplary—to punish the defendant for his wrongdoing.

In modern times, however, the action has taken a new form—a claim for damages against the co-respondent—and the courts have disclaimed any idea of punishing the co-respondent. It has been laid down that the damages are only to be given as a compensation to the husband for the loss of his wife. He gets more damages if she is a good wife and housekeeper than if she is not. This is a practical point of view which on the whole works justice. Even when so modified, however, the very idea of awarding damages is now being called in question. If wives are to be regarded not as chattels but as women with wills of their own, then the wife who commits adultery is as much at fault as the co-respondent. The husband can divorce her, just as in the converse case she can divorce him, but a money award is now coming to be considered by some to be just as inappropriate against a co-respondent as against a named woman.

HER RIGHTS OF PROPERTY

Now let me turn from the wife's personal position to her ownership of property. We know that in the marriage service it is the man who assures the woman that " with all my worldly goods I thee endow "; but the law did the exact opposite. Upon marriage all the woman's goods and chattels, and all her money, automatically belonged to the man save for her own personal clothing and paraphernalia. If her parents or friends gave her wedding presents, such as a writing desk or a pair of candlesticks, they belonged to the husband. If during the marriage she went out to work, all that she earned belonged automatically to her husband. Just think what great power this gave to him, and how dependent it made her. She had to go to him, on bended knee, whenever she wanted to buy anything even with her own money or her own earnings. If she left him, even for good cause, she had no right to any maintenance even out of her own funds. The only remedy which the common law gave her was that she could pledge his credit for necessaries, but even then she had to find some tradesman who would supply her—and none might be willing to do so. Most tradesmen, however keen they were to do business, also wished to be sure of being paid. They did not wish to be involved in a lawsuit as to whether the wife was entitled to pledge her husband's credit or not. If they were unwilling to accept the husband's credit, it was useless for the wife to pledge her own. She had no power to contract on her own behalf, because she was one with her husband and could agree to nothing apart from him. Moreover, she had no property or money with which to honour any contract which she might make. She was in a parlous plight.

Some relief was given by the courts of equity to the

daughters of the rich. Their parents made marriage settlements and trusts in which they settled money for the separate use of the daughters when they married; and they made provision whereby a married daughter received only the income, and could not touch the capital, so that, although it was out of her reach, it was out of her husband's reach also. These benefits did not extend to daughters whose parents were less well off and could not afford a marriage settlement.

DISADVANTAGES FOR HUSBANDS

I must notice one disadvantage which came to the husband by taking all his wife's property. He became liable to pay damages for all the wrongs which she committed. If she slandered her neighbour across the tea-table, the husband had to foot the bill. If she was involved in a road accident owing to her own fault, the husband had to pay compensation to those whom she injured. This was all very well in the case of those husbands whose wives did bring them money on marriage, but it was rather hard on those husbands whose wives came with nothing. That injustice has been remedied by statute, but I must mention, however, another disadvantage which still remains on the husband. The husband is liable to pay tax on her income as well as on his own. For tax purposes her income is regarded as his. I make no comment on this save that if a man and woman should live together without going through the ceremony of marriage—with the woman simply changing her name to his by deed poll, as she can easily do—they can have all the benefits of marriage without the tax which marriage imposes.

DISABILITIES SWEPT AWAY

Now by a series of Acts of Parliament starting in 1870 and finishing in 1949, all the disabilities of wives in regard to property have been swept away. A married woman is now entitled to her own property and earnings, just as her husband is entitled to his. Her stocks and shares remain hers. Her wedding presents are hers. Her earnings are hers. She can deal with all her property as fully as any man. She can no longer be restrained from touching the capital. She can make contracts on her own account, and can sue and be sued upon them by herself alone. She is liable for her own wrongdoing and her husband is not. Her equality in property matters has now by statute been made complete.

THE 1882 ACT

The great emancipation statute was the Married Women's Property Act, 1882, but it took a long time for this statute to have full effect. Despite the 1882 Act the judges for a long time tended to pay too much heed to old precedents decided before 1882.

They did not modify them to suit the new conditions. It is only recently that the position has been put right. The vexed matter of the housekeeping allowance is a good illustration. In 1856—a quarter of a century before the 1882 Act—the courts decided that any savings which a wife made from her housekeeping allowance belonged to her husband absolutely. She had no equity to say that they belonged to her for her separate use. This was understandable in those days when the wife was regarded by the law as the chattel of her husband and not as a partner. But the decision was carried over into modern times when a married woman has become the equal of her husband. Only 10 years ago the Court of Appeal held that any money which the wife saved from the housekeeping allowance belonged to her husband absolutely.[9]

[9] *Blackwell* v. *Blackwell* [1943] 2 All E.R. 579.

This was followed four years ago by a case where the husband and wife jointly made a winning forecast in a football pool and bought some furniture with the prize money. The stake money was paid out of the housekeeping allowance. It was held that the husband was entitled to the furniture unless the wife could prove a contract by him to give it to her.[10] That she could not do because these matters are not made the subject of a formal contract when parties are living together.

THE NEW PARTNERSHIP

The idea underlying those two cases is that the husband is the owner of the money he earns and of the proceeds of it: and that the wife must be considered as handling it merely as his agent. That idea is now being ousted by the modern idea that husband and wife are partners in all affairs which are their common concern. He goes out to work so as to earn money for the partnership. She stays at home so as to run the family side of the business. If she by good housekeeping manages to save money for the partnership, it belongs to the partnership jointly. If he or she buys furniture for the home, it also belongs to them jointly. Some things are, of course, separate property. Each owns his own clothes and personal belongings. Each owns his own investments. But things which are intended to be a continuing provision for both, such as the house and furniture, belong to both jointly.

THE " RIMMER " CASE

Such is the modern idea and such is the trend of the recent cases. The Court of Appeal has now laid it down that, when a question of property arises between husband and wife, it is not to be solved by applying the rules of

---

[10] *Hoddinott* v. *Hoddinott* [1949] 2 K.B. 406.

law or equity which are applied to strangers. When a house or furniture is bought, the court is not to ask itself simply which of them provided the money or which of them made the contract of purchase. The court recognises that house or furniture is often provided by their joint efforts or at any rate provided for the use of them both jointly, so that they are in effect joint owners of it. If they afterwards separate, or are divorced, the only fair thing is to treat them as joint owners and divide it equally between them. A case decided only last year is a good illustration of this new approach. The husband and the wife both went out to work. He allowed her £4 a week housekeeping allowance. She earned £3 10s. a week herself. She paid all the household expenses out of the housekeeping allowance and saved her own earnings for herself. The house stood in the husband's name. She paid the current instalments to the building society out of the housekeeping allowance, but she paid off the capital out of her own earnings. They afterwards separated and the question was to whom the house belonged. If they had been regarded as strangers, the husband would have had the better legal title because the house stood in his name and he had from the beginning made himself responsible to the building society: but the wife had the better equitable title because she had provided most of the capital repayments out of her own earnings. The court held that neither of them had a superior claim to the other. The question could not be decided according to the legal or equitable title as it would be decided between strangers. It had to be decided on the broad principle that between husband and wife, when the title to property is doubtful, it should be held to belong to both jointly.[11]

[11] *Rimmer* v. *Rimmer* [1953] 1 Q.B. 63.

As a result of that decision there is no longer any just ground for reproaching the law as being behind the times in this important subject. Those who have been urging Parliament to intervene may find that it is no longer necessary. The courts have not so much changed the law. They have only expounded it. In the 1882 Act Parliament gave the courts a wide discretion to decide questions of property between husband and wife " as they thought fit." The courts are now beginning to exercise that discretion in accordance with modern conceptions of the relationship of husband and wife, without being tied to the old notions on the matter.

DESERTED WIVES

A similar development has taken place about the position of wives who have been deserted by their husbands. Many people used to think that the law was out of date on this matter. They have presented Bills to Parliament suggesting that the law should be altered. But if they keep in touch with current decisions they will find that most of the problems have already been solved.

Only a few years ago it was commonly believed that a wife, who was living in a house which belonged to her husband, was in no better position than a servant or a licensee with no right to stay a moment longer than he permitted her to stay. The lawyers then looked at husband and wife as they would at strangers. The husband had the legal title to the house. The wife had no estate or interest in it. She must therefore go at his bidding. This was obviously most unjust, especially in a case where the husband had deserted his wife, leaving her in the matrimonial home. It meant that he could soon afterwards turn her out so that he could sell it at a profit with vacant possession : or so that he could return to live in the house with the woman with whom he was committing adultery. The way in which in these circumstances the courts have protected the deserted wife is a most instructive chapter of recent legal history. It shows that in our day, as in former days, the substantive law is often to be found secreted in the interstices of legal procedure.

PROTECTION AGAINST HER HUSBAND

It started in a case in 1942 where a husband brought an action in the county court to eject his wife from the matrimonial home. The only defence she put up was that she was a tenant of her husband. The defence failed and she was ordered to go. Her lawyers did not take a point which would have been decisive in her favour. Lord Justice Goddard first mentioned it in the Court of Appeal.[12] It was this: At common law a husband could not sue his wife at all, because husband and wife were one. Even since 1882 he cannot sue his wife for a tort, that is for a wrong done. He cannot therefore sue her in ejectment or trespass because those are both torts. The only remedy is to apply to the court under the special procedure prescribed under the 1882 Act. Once he is forced back to that procedure, he is no longer in a commanding position, because, under the special provisions of the statute, the court is given a wide discretion to make " such order as it thinks fit." The procedural point thus suggested by Lord Goddard has borne much fruit. A husband who has deserted his wife cannot now turn her out unless the court in its discretion makes an order against her, and the court, I need hardly say, will not as a rule eject her unless she has somewhere else to go and the husband provides

12 In *Bramwell* v. *Bramwell* [1942] 1 K.B. at p. 374.

her with proper maintenance.[13]   When this procedure is looked at from the wife's point of view, it means that she has a right to stay until the court orders her out.

PROTECTION AGAINST THE LANDLORD

The next step was to protect the wife not only against her husband but also against the landlord.   The tenancy of the matrimonial home is usually in the husband's name.   When he deserts his wife, he often tries to get rid of his responsibilities to the landlord by giving notice of intention to quit or by submitting to an order for possession.   Sometimes the landlord himself serves a notice to quit and tries to get the wife out.   On account of these difficulties there are many who suggest that a deserted wife should be allowed to take over the tenancy of the matrimonial home.   The advocates of this course will also find their problems have already been solved.   It has been done in this way.   In the old days a deserted wife was given by law an irrevocable authority to pledge her husband's credit for necessaries.   That used to be applied only for food and clothes, but it can also be applied to lodging.   One of the most obvious necessaries for a wife is to have a roof over her head.   A deserted wife has been held therefore to have an irrevocable authority to continue the tenancy in the husband's name.   If the house is within the Rent Acts, as it usually is, she is entitled to continue on there herself so long as she pays the rent and performs the conditions of the tenancy.[14] She ought to be able to get the money to pay the rent. She can go to the court and ask for maintenance from her husband to cover it, or she may go out to work and earn money herself.   This seems fair to both.   The wife

/ [13] *H.* v. *H.*, 63 T.L.R. 645.
[14] *Old Gate Estates* v. *Alexander* [1950] 1 K.B. 311; *Middleton* v. *Baldock* [1950] 1 K.B. 657.

is allowed to stay on so long as she pays the rent. The landlord does not suffer because he is in as good a position as if the husband himself had stayed on in the house.

PROTECTION AGAINST SUCCESSORS

The right of the deserted wife has recently been extended so as to apply not only as against her husband but also against his successors in title who take with notice of her right. In one case the husband owned the house and later became bankrupt. The trustee in bankruptcy sought to evict the wife because he wanted to sell the house with vacant possession. The court held that the trustee in bankruptcy was in no better position than the husband.[15] In another case the husband sold the house to a friend for a small sum so that the friend could get her out. The friend failed also.[16] Even if the wife herself sins she does not necessarily lose her right. In one case, after the husband had deserted her for some years, she started to live with the lodger and had a child by him. Yet it was held that the landlord could not turn her out so long as she paid the rent.[17] There is one definite limit, however, to the right of a deserted wife. It ceases if she divorces her husband. If she wishes to stay on in the house, she must arrange that with her husband in the divorce proceedings and get the Divorce Court to sanction it. Otherwise after the divorce she may find that she has to go.[18]

All this shows how the courts, in their daily task of deciding concrete cases can and do work out a coherent body of law to meet the needs of modern times. Contrast this with the way of Parliament. Bills may be

---

[15] *Bendall* v. *McWhirter* [1952] 2 Q.B. 466.
[16] *Ferris* v. *Weaven* [1952] 2 All E.R. 233.
[17] *Wabe* v. *Taylor* [1952] 2 K.B. 735.
[18] *Vaughan* v. *Vaughan* [1953] 1 W.L.R. 236.

introduced; committees or commissions may be appointed to inquire; eventually a statute may be passed. This does not afford a remedy for the injustices of the past. It only gives a remedy for the future; and the remedy is not always a happy one. The courts are then concerned only with the words which Parliament has used. Words are the masters: and there is no telling what the ingenuity of lawyers may not do with words.

HER EQUALITY IN OTHER MATTERS

In full accord with all I have said is the position of children. In former times the law gave the father full rights over the children of the marriage. They were considered as his property. If the parties separated and differed as to who should have the children the father had the superior claim. If they quarrelled as to whether the children should be brought up as Roman Catholics or as Protestants, the father had the right to say which it should be. This was not altered until 1925 when it was ordained by Parliament that whenever any question arose about a child the father had no superior right to the mother and that the paramount consideration was always the welfare of the child.

Even with regard to divorce there was until recently serious inequality. When the courts of this country in 1857 were first authorised to grant divorces so as to permit remarriage, a husband could divorce his wife for adultery alone, but she could not divorce him unless he had been guilty not only of adultery but also of cruelty or desertion. In short, adultery by a woman was a grave offence leading to divorce, but by a man it was a mere peccadillo which the wife must overlook. This cynical distinction was indefensible. A man is not entitled to expect of his wife a higher standard than he is prepared to observe himself. But it was not until 1923 that this was recognised. Now, of course, a woman is entitled to divorce her husband on the same grounds as he is entitled to divorce her.

Not only in domestic law but also in constitutional law equality has been achieved. Before 1918 men alone could vote. Then women over 30 were allowed to vote, and it was not until 1928 that women could vote at the age of 21, the same as men. Meanwhile, however, in 1919 the Sex Disqualification Act was passed which specifically enacted that women should not be disqualified by their sex from any office or post, profession or vocation, or from jury service. So we find them now fully enfranchised save for sitting in the House of Lords and taking Holy Orders.

CONCLUSION

Gathering now the threads together, let us see how in law women have gained equality with men. A wife's right to be regarded as a partner and not as a subordinate of her husband was achieved by a series of judicial decisions from 1891 to 1952. Her right to own her own property, earn her own money, make her own contracts, and to sue and be sued alone, was gained by a series of Acts of Parliament from 1870 to 1949. Her right to vote, to occupy public positions, to enter the professions, to serve on juries, and so forth, dates only from 1919. Her right to divorce on equal grounds with her husband was given in 1923. Her right to an equal voice in matters concerning the children was attained in 1925. Later Acts have tidied up the position in several respects. It can now be said of the Englishwoman that her situation, whether married or unmarried, has become one of great personal and proprietary independence.

As against all this independence, however, it must be remembered that the husband still remains in law under great obligations. He is in law liable to maintain his wife. He must go out to work to support her, but she is not bound to work to support him. She can still pledge his credit for necessaries, but he cannot pledge hers, no matter how rich she is and how much she earns. She can sue him in the courts for the protection of her property, but he cannot sue her except in an indirect way.

If it comes to a separation or divorce, the courts will enforce his obligation to maintain her, unless she has sufficient means of her own or she has forfeited her right by her own conduct, and he is, as a rule, compelled to pay the costs. If she is the " spoilt darling " of the law, he is the patient pack-horse. By putting these obligations on the husband, however, the law recognises the natural state of affairs whereby the man's proper function is to work to provide for his wife and family, and the woman's proper place is to look after the home and bring up the children. If a wife is to do these things properly, she has usually to withdraw from the money market and find her reward in the home—a reward which is much more worth while.

THE INFLUENCE OF RELIGION

In primitive societies, the influence of religion on law was obvious, but it is not so obvious in modern societies. In primitive communities religion, morals and law were indistinguishably mixed together. In the Ten Commandments, for instance, you find the first Commandment which is *religious* : " God spake these words and said, ' I am the Lord thy God : Thou shalt have none other Gods but me.' " You find the fifth Commandment which is a *moral* precept : " Honour thy father and thy mother : that thy days may be long in the land which the Lord thy God giveth thee." You find the eighth Commandment which is a *legal* duty : " Thou shalt not steal." This intermingling is typical of all early communities. The severance of the three ideas—of law from morality, and of religion from law—belongs very distinctly to the later stages of mental progress.

This severance has gone a great way. Many people now think that religion and law have nothing in common. The law, they say, governs our dealings with our fellows : whereas religion concerns our dealings with God. Likewise they hold that law has nothing to do with morality. It lays down rigid rules which must be obeyed without questioning whether they are right or wrong. Its function is to keep order, not to do justice.

The severance has, I think, gone much too far. Although religion, law and morals can be separated, they are nevertheless still very much dependent on each other. Without religion there can be no morality : and without morality there can be no law. I will try to show you how many of the fundamental principles of our law have been derived from the Christian religion :

and in so doing I will try to indicate how they are
challenged by a changing world which knows no religion,
or at any rate treats religion as something which is of
no moment in practical affairs.

TRUTH

Let me start first with truth. No one here doubts, I
hope, that it is his duty to tell the truth. Nevertheless if
your actions were governed by expediency alone, without
regard to the precepts of law, religion or morals, you
would soon find that there is as much to be said for lying
as there is for telling the truth. You would discard the
old saying that " honesty is the best policy " as a maxim
fit for fools but not for clever people like yourself. If it
were necessary in order to attain your ends that you
should tell a lie, then tell it you would : for the end would
justify the means. For instance, if your friend was
charged with being drunk in charge of a car, and it
would help him for you to say he was sober, then say
it you would, although you knew he was drunk.

The reason why that reasoning is not acceptable to
most of us is, I believe, because we have been taught
the contrary from our mother's knee. The Christian
religion has always stressed the importance of truth,
absolute truth, in all our dealings. Just as the psalmist
commends the man who " speaketh the truth from his
heart," [1] so also St. Paul enjoins the early Christians
in these words : " Wherefore putting away lying, speak
every man truth with his neighbour : for we are members
one of another." [2] If there is one thing that gives rise
to more resentment than anything else it is to be
deceived—to be told a lie. It is an affront to the whole

[1] Psalm xv, 2.
[2] Ephesians iv, 25.

personality.   Just as we do not wish others to deceive us, so we should not deceive them.

" PIOUS FRAUD "

Some theologians have argued that it is permissible to tell a lie for a just cause.   The Roman Catholic Church itself did so at one time.   For instance they invented legendary incidents relating to the life of Our Lord and the saints, and portrayed them as true.   It was done with the best of motives so as to help people to believe, but nevertheless it was a fraud.   Hence the phrase " pious fraud " which has become part of our language.   A parallel in modern times is when doctors sometimes deceive their patients because they believe it is for their good to do so.   I am not sure, however, that it is ever permissible for any man to tell a lie to his neighbour. St. Augustine held that the duty of truth is absolute and he would permit no exceptions to it : and he gave as a sufficient reason that, by lying, eternal life is lost.   In modern times Kant and other philosophers take the view that truth is absolute.   What then, you may ask, is to be said about stratagems made by our military men for deceiving the enemy ?   Some of them are downright lies but no one sees any wrong in them.   On the contrary it is matter for congratulation when they succeed.   The answer for the Christian is, I suggest, that an enemy, who is seeking to destroy you, can hardly be considered your neighbour.

THE TAKING OF AN OATH

Turning now to the law, it has insisted upon the truth being told on all occasions without exception.   It is not difficult to see the reason why.   Justice cannot be done unless the truth be known.   The judges have to rely on the statements of witnesses. If it were permissible for a witness to tell a lie to help his friend, it would be the end of any attempt to do justice. I must remark, however, in parenthesis that this reasoning assumes that the law itself is just, and that the judges decide the cases justly. If the law is harsh and unjust, or is unjustly administered, then witnesses may be tempted to permit themselves a " pious fraud." In the old days when stealing anything worth more than 40 shillings was punishable with death, a jury solemnly found that a £5 bank-note was only worth 39s.: and no one thought it reprehensible. Hence the importance of seeing that the law is not only certain, but also that it is just.

On the assumption that the law is just, the judges insist on absolute truth : and to emphasise its importance, they require the witness to take an oath that he will tell the truth. There is nothing, perhaps, in our legal procedure which so clearly shows the influence of religion as the taking of an oath. Ever since there has been a system of law in this country, it has proceeded on the footing that each man believes in God. And it still proceeds on that footing. When a man goes into the witness box the first thing he has to do is to take the oath. Silence is demanded in court to emphasise the solemnity of what he is about to do. The witness takes the book in his hand and says these words : " I swear by Almighty God that the evidence I shall give shall be the truth, the whole truth, and nothing but the truth." The book that is handed to him, unless he asks for another, is the New Testament. By that oath the witness is not merely making a solemn affirmation to the judge. He is binding himself to God that he will tell the truth : and before God there is no room for half-truths or pious frauds. This is well known to ordinary folk who come to give evidence. Some of the more emphatic sort have been known to protest too much the truth of their answer by adding " May God strike me dead if I have told a lie." It is recorded that on one occasion on the Western Circuit a witness who made such an exclamation, did fall down dead, and a stone is set up to note the fact. Witnesses of other religious faiths take the oath according to the form of their own religion, but it must always be an oath which is binding on their conscience.

NO HALF-TRUTHS

So much for witnesses. But the law does not only insist on people telling the truth on oath. It insists on truth in all affairs of life where one person acts on the word of another. There is nothing upon which the law is more strict. It allows no evasions. Half-truths are condemned as much as real falsehoods. If a statement is literally true but conveys a wrong impression because of what is left unsaid, that is fraud, as the late Lord Kylsant once found out to his cost. He had inserted in a company's prospectus figures for the years which had shown profits but omitted those for the years which had shown losses, and the net result was to make the company's position look much better than it was. He was sent to prison for 12 months.[3] The principle underlying all the rules of law on these subjects, fraud, misrepresentation, estoppel and the like is this: No man shall get a benefit from a lie if the law can prevent him. No excuse or justification is permitted. It is not allowable to tell a lie in order to achieve a just result. A good end does not justify a bad means.[4]

The law therefore is sound enough on this point: but what I would observe is that law is not sufficient by itself.

[3] *R.* v. *Kylsant* [1932] 1 K.B. 442.
[4] *Hobbs* v. *Pinling* [1929] 2 K.B. at p. 53.

If the people have not true religion, then all the ordinances of the law are of little use. May not this be the reason why honesty has declined in recent times? Many people do not seem nowadays to pay much regard to the sanctity of an oath. They say that which they think helps their case, whether it be true or not.

GOOD FAITH

Akin to truth is the requirement of good faith. Just as you must tell the truth, so you must keep your promises. The just man in the Psalms is not only " he that hath used no deceit on his tongue," but also " he that sweareth unto his neighbour and disappointeth him not: though it were to his own hindrance." [5] This precept finds its place in the law also. Our law of contract has passed through many phases. At one time promises were not binding unless they were made in the form of a covenant under seal. Later on they were not binding unless there was consideration for them, that is, something given or done as the price for them. Nowadays nearly all formalities have been eliminated. If a man makes a promise which is intended to be binding and to be acted upon by the party to whom it is addressed, then once he has acted upon it, it is enforceable at law.

STANDARDISED CONTRACTS

So far so good. But the law on this matter has on occasions over-reached itself. The best instance is perhaps the way it has treated standardised contracts. Large concerns, such as hire-purchase companies, insurance companies, and others often issue printed forms containing many conditions of contract. The small individual member of the public has no choice but either to accept them or else go without the benefit of any

[5] Psalm xv, 3, 5,

contract at all. More often than not, he does not read them, and even if he did, he would probably not understand them. Yet he is bound by their conditions as if he had deliberately promised to fulfil them. Again, when it comes to the interpretation of contracts, the law holds the man bound to the letter of his contract although unforeseen circumstances have arisen which make it unjust to enforce it against him. If he protests and says " I could not have foreseen it," the law replies : " It is your own fault. You ought to have put in a saving clause to protect yourself." This harsh ruling is not in accordance with the view of St. Thomas Aquinas who would hold him excused. If good faith is required in a person who gives a promise, so it should be in a person who takes the benefit of it. He should not enforce it in circumstances which it was never intended to cover.

Just as the law has over-reached itself with contracts, so it has also with the interpretation of statutes. If a situation arises which Parliament never intended, and a strict interpretation of the statute gives rise to injustice, nevertheless the law cannot, or will not, lift a finger to help. It is not for the judges to fill in the gaps in the Acts of Parliament.

" THE LETTER KILLETH "

I cannot help thinking that this literal interpretation of contracts or statutes is a departure from real truth. It makes words the masters of men instead of their servants. If you read your New Testament, you will find that there is nothing more condemned than the insistence on the letter. A good instance is the case about the Sabbath day. The fourth Commandment ordained that on it " thou shalt do no manner of work." It so happened that, on one Sabbath day, as the disciples went through the cornfields, they began to pluck the ears of corn.   The Pharisees said to our Lord, "Why do they on the Sabbath day that which is not lawful?"   He replied: "The Sabbath was made for man, and not man for the Sabbath." [6]   And St. Paul put the principle succinctly when he said "the letter killeth but the spirit giveth life." [7]   That precept was at one time remembered in our English law.   In the days when the Bible was first put into English the judges laid down rules which were undoubtedly influenced by the Bible teaching.   The statutes were to be interpreted, not only according to the language used, but also with regard to the mischief which Parliament sought to remedy, so as to give "force and life" to the intention of the legislature.   Those words were clearly taken from the epistle "the spirit giveth life."   But in the nineteenth century that broad view was supplanted by a rule which Baron Parke described as a golden rule.   He said that statutes, and indeed all documents, were to be interpreted according to the grammatical and ordinary sense of the words.   Even if the grammatical meaning gave rise to unjust results which Parliament never intended, nevertheless the grammatical meaning must prevail.   This means I fear that the judges are too often inclined to fold their hands and blame the legislature, when really they ought to set to work and give the words a reasonable meaning, even if this does involve a departure from the letter of them.   By so doing they are more likely to find the truth.

"LOVE THY NEIGHBOUR"

Let us now turn from truth to justice.   No one here doubts, I hope, that it is his duty to be just and fair in

[6] St. Mark ii, 23–28.
[7] II Corinthians 3, 6.

all his dealings. But our conception of justice is only the Christian teaching of love. Such at least was the view of William Temple, Archbishop of Canterbury, one of the greatest thinkers of the present century. " It is axiomatic," he said, " that love should be the predominant Christian impulse and that the primary form of love in social organisation is justice." The Christian standpoint is summed up in the gospel when a certain lawyer asked our Lord, " Master, what shall I do to inherit eternal life ? " He said unto him " What is written in the law ? How readest thou ? " And he answering said " Thou shalt love the Lord thy God with all thy heart, and with all thy soul and with all thy mind, and thy neighbour as thyself." And he said unto him " Thou hast answered right: this do and thou shalt live." This precept—love towards God and love towards your neighbour —is a precept of religion, but nevertheless in many affairs of life, love can only find expression through justice. William Temple gave this illustration: " Imagine a Trade Union Committee negotiating with an Employers' Federation in an industrial crisis on the verge of a strike. This Committee is to be actuated by love. Oh, yes, by all means, but towards whom ? Are they to love the workers or the employers ? Of course—both. But then that will not help them much to determine what terms ought to be either proposed or accepted. . . . Love, in fact, finds its primary expression through justice which, in the field of industrial disputes, means in practice that each side should state its case as strongly as it can before the most impartial tribunal available, with determination to accept the award of that tribunal. At least that puts the two parties on a level, and is to that extent in accordance with the command ' Thou shalt love thy neighbour as thyself.' " [8]

[8] Temple: *Christianity and the Social Order.*

Such being the view of the theologian, let me now turn
to the judge, whose task it is to be the tribunal. He
must do justice between the parties. But how is he to
know what is justice? Let me tell you how one great
judge answered it. It arose in a case where a manufacturer of ginger beer had made it so carelessly that he
left a snail in one of the bottles. He sold it as part of a
consignment to a shopkeeper, who in turn sold a bottle
to a man whose wife drank it and was injured. At one
time the law held that the manufacturer was not liable
to pay any compensation because he had made no contract with the ultimate purchaser or his wife. But in
1932 the House of Lords held that the manufacturer was
liable. In a judgment of great importance in the law,
Lord Atkin took the Christian precept as the underlying
basis of the decision in these words: " The rule that you
are to love your neighbour becomes in law you must not
injure your neighbour: and the lawyer's question ' Who
is my neighbour? ' receives a restricted reply. You
must take reasonable care to avoid acts or omissions
which you can reasonably foresee would be likely to
injure your neighbour. Who then in law is my neighbour? The answer seems to be—persons who are so
closely and directly affected by my act that I ought
reasonably to have them in contemplation as being so
affected when I am directing my mind to the acts or
omissions which are called in question." [9]

It is, I suggest to you, a most significant thing that
a great judge should draw his principles of law, or rather
his principles of justice, from the Christian commandment of love. I do not know where else he is to find
them. Some people speak of natural justice as though

[9] *Donoghue* v. *Stevenson* [1932] A.C. 562, 580.

it was a thing well recognisable by anyone, whatever his training and upbringing. But I am quite sure that our conception of it is due entirely to our habits of thought through many generations. The common law of England has been moulded for centuries by judges who have been brought up in the Christian faith. The precepts of religion, consciously or unconsciously, have been their guide in the administration of justice.

BASIS OF CIVIL WRONGS

Perhaps the best illustration of this is the law of this country about civil wrongs. At one time the ruling principle (derived from Roman law) was that a person was not liable to pay damages unless he had been guilty of some fault, such as some negligence, some invasion on another's property, or the like. The underlying justification for this rule was that damages were a deterrent. If he was made to pay damages, he was not so likely to commit the same fault again. But those who put forward this view always had great difficulty in explaining why a master should be liable to pay damages for his servant's fault. Nowadays (save for rare exceptions), damages are not regarded as a deterrent or a punishment, but rather as compensation for harm done. The law proceeds, I suggest, on the Christian principle: If you love your neighbour, you will take care not to injure him. And if perchance you should by your negligence (or even by the negligence of your servants) do him some damage, you will wish to compensate him. If you do not do so, the law will require you to do what you ought to have done willingly, but it will not go further and punish you. It will not exact anything in the nature of vengeance or retribution. If proof of this were needed, it is to be found in the fact that you can insure yourself against any damages you have to pay. This means that the law does not insist on the compensation coming from your own pocket. It is sufficient if your insurance company pays. It is obvious that, when you have covered your liability by insurance, the award of damages has no punitive or deterrent effect on you. It is a compensation for the injured party and nothing else. Once this is appreciated, you can understand why a master should pay compensation for his servant's fault. The servant is doing the master's business and the master should be answerable for the servant's act as if it were his own. A noteworthy illustration of the modern approach is to be found in the case of a guest of a Brighton hotel who got annoyed with the manager and made a brutal assault on him. He was taken before the criminal courts and found to be insane. He could not therefore be said to be at fault but nevertheless he was ordered by a civil court to pay compensation to the injured manager.

PUNISHMENT FOR CRIME

Whilst civil wrongs are thus redressed by compensation, nevertheless there still remain all the criminal wrongs which must be met by punishment. The command that you are to love your neighbour does not mean that those who do wrong should not be punished. In the Epistle of St. Peter it is said that governors are sent by God " for the punishment of evil-doers." What then is the right way to punish them? What is to be done with people who are enemies of society, men who prey upon it by theft and fraud, men who assault innocent women and children, men who are murderers? At one time the law held that they should be exterminated. Nearly all serious offences were punishable by death. But under the influence of a more humane jurisprudence, or rather

I would say of a more Christian outlook, capital punishment has been abolished in all cases except murder or treason: and there are many who would abolish it even in those cases. The principal object of punishment is now generally accepted to be the reformation of the criminal: and the Criminal Justice Act, 1948 is a notable step to this end.

In any discussion of punishment it is important to recognise, as Christianity does, that society itself is responsible for the conditions which makes men criminals. It is a commonplace that broken homes produce juvenile delinquents. The child who has lost his sense of security feels that he must fight for his interests in a hostile world. He becomes anti-social and finally criminal. The broken home from which he comes is only too often a reflection on society itself, a society which has failed to respect the sanctity of marriage, a society which has failed to maintain its standards of morality, a society which has lost its religion. When we try to reform the criminal, we are only treating the symptoms of the disease. We are not tackling the cause of it. The best way to deal with it is to reform society itself: and in this regard, I need hardly say that the leaders of society have an especial responsibility. It is disturbing to find how many broken homes, how many matrimonial offences, exist among those in high positions.

INDIVIDUAL RESPONSIBILITY

Nevertheless, although society itself is largely responsible, neither religion nor the law excuses the criminal himself. Christianity has always stressed the responsibility of each individual for his own wrong-doing. It does not say to him " Poor thing, you couldn't help it, could you? You came from a broken home and nothing else could be expected." That would lead him to believe that he is more sinned against than sinning and implies that strenuous moral effort on his part is unnecessary or futile. The Christian approach is different. It allows no easy excuse but demands of everyone that he must repent and reform. You will remember the opening verse of the Book of Common Prayer: " When the wicked man turneth away from his wickedness that he hath committed, and doeth that which is lawful and right, he shall save his soul alive ": and as it is said in the Gospel of St. Luke " There is joy in the presence of God over one sinner that repenteth."

THE GUILTY MIND

In order to hold a person individually responsible for his crime, so as to be liable to punishment, it is obviously necessary that he should have a guilty mind. This requirement is first found in St. Augustine's sermons where it is said that you are not guilty of perjury unless you have a guilty mind. Thence it found its place in the laws of Henry I when it was laid down as law that *reum non facit nisi mens rea*, that is, there is no guilt unless there is a guilty mind. That has been the rule of English law from that time to this. In order that an act should be punishable, it must be morally blameworthy. It must be a sin.

INSANITY AND CRIME

When you speak of a guilty mind, however, the question immediately arises, How are you to deal with those who are not of sound mind? At first sight the law seems clear enough. If a man is insane when he commits a crime, he cannot be punished, because he cannot be said to have a guilty mind. If he becomes insane after he has committed a crime, he cannot be hanged because he must not be deprived of the opportunity of repenting. But the difficulty arises when you ask, What is insanity ? Time and time again it happens that a jury find a man guilty of wilful murder whilst of sound mind, but nevertheless he is afterwards reprieved on the ground that he has since been found to be insane. It is the accepted practice, authorised by statute, for the Home Secretary to appoint two doctors to examine him. If the doctors find him to be insane, he is reprieved. In theory the finding of the doctors does not contradict the verdict of the jury. The jury are only concerned with his state of mind when he committed the crime : whereas the doctors are concerned with it at the time they examined him. If he is insane at that time, he must not be hanged. As matter of common sense the findings of the jury and the doctors ought usually to coincide. One realises, of course, that they may differ. A man may be so mentally affected by his trial and sentence that he becomes insane afterwards : but that is a rare thing. His state of mind is usually the same throughout. The reason why the Home Office doctors so often find him to be insane is that they adopt a different test of insanity from that which the jury have to apply. Let me tell you about these tests because they can both be traced to the Christian conception of individual responsibility, but each regarding it in a different light.

THE MCNAGHTEN RULES

The test applied by the jury in judging insanity is the test laid down by the judges in 1843 in the McNaghten Rules. These lay the emphasis on the man's knowledge, not on his will-power. If he was so mad that he did not know what he was doing at all, any more than a sleep-walker does, then he is excused; or if he did not know that what he was doing was wrong, as if he was under a delusion that he was being attacked in war by the enemy, then also he is excused. But if he knew what he was doing and that it was wrong, then he is not excused. It may be that he was driven on by some blind impulse; nevertheless if he knew it was wrong, he is not excused in law.

The test applied by the doctors in judging insanity denies the distinction between a man's knowledge and his will-power. If the man is what they call a psychopathic personality, driven on by some morbid urge which he has not the will-power to resist, then the doctors hold that he should be excused, even though he knows perfectly well that he is doing wrong.

THE STRAFFEN CASE

The difference of approach is well illustrated by two recent cases of which you will all have read in the newspapers. A young man called Straffen strangled two small girls. He was arrested, but when brought up for trial the doctors said he was unfit to plead, and accordingly he was detained as a lunatic in the Broadmoor Asylum. He behaved himself well in the asylum, but one day he escaped for a few hours and strangled another small girl. He was again arrested and brought up for trial. This time the doctors said he was fit to plead. The defence of insanity was raised, but the jury rejected it and found him guilty of wilful murder. Later he was reprieved on the ground, no doubt, that the Home Office doctors found him to be insane.

I expect that the jury reasoned something like this : "This man is better out of the way. He is subject to such dreadful impulses that it is better for the community that he should be put to death rather than there should be any risk of another escape. This should be done, not so much to punish him as to protect the community." Whereas the view of the doctors presumably was: "This man is not responsible for his actions. He is subject to impulses which he cannot resist. He should be regarded as insane and should not be punished."

In contrast to the Straffen case, you must notice the case of Miles Giffard, a young man who murdered both his father and his mother and pushed the bodies in a wheelbarrow over the edge of a cliff. He did it because they wouldn't let him have the use of a car or some other quite inadequate reason. There was a history of mental instability in him and in the family. The defence of insanity was raised but the jury found him guilty. This time the Home Secretary did not grant a reprieve and Giffard was hanged. This case seems to show that there are some crimes which shock the public conscience so much that ordinary members of the public say that the murderer is better out of the way, even though he was mentally unstable. It is not so much a matter of punishing him. It is rather the community defending itself. It is said that Giffard went to his death repentant for his sins and, it may be hoped, at peace with his Maker.

A PROBLEM OF ETHICS

It is worth pausing for a moment at this point, because those two cases illustrate one of the most difficult problems of Christian ethics of our time. It is this: Is it permissible for society to exterminate those who have an irresistible impulse to murder? A similar problem arises about sterilisation. If a man is subject to mad sexual impulses which causes him to inflict grave injury on innocent women, is it permissible to sterilise him? or alternatively to keep him in prison indefinitely until he is past the age when he will do such things? In Denmark they have now a law whereby a sexual offender is sentenced to prison for as long as the State thinks fit to keep him there, but he can obtain his freedom by submitting to sterilisation. In England we have never gone so far. We do not permit sterilisation of the unfit. I expect this has its origin in the sanctity which Christianity attaches to human life. Just as life itself is sacred, so are the means of producing it: and it is not to be taken away except by Him who is the Creator of it. The danger is, of course, that once authority is given to society to exterminate, to sterilise or to intern indefinitely some of its members, you may find that those who are in authority in the State may use it, as the Nazis did, against those whom they dislike. I offer no solution except to suggest that true Christianity should try to strike a correct balance between the individual and the society of which he forms part.

MAN AND THE STATE

I have now told you all I wish of Truth and Justice : but these lead me on to consider the relations between man and the State. Truth and Justice do not exist in a vacuum. They exist in a society of human beings, in short, in a State : and a State can be so organised that Truth and Justice can disappear, or at any rate be stifled. What does Christianity say about this? Let me take for an answer again the words of William Temple : " The primary principle of Christian ethics and Christian politics must be respect for every person simply as a person. If each man and woman is a child of God, whom God loves and for whom Christ died, then there is in each a work absolutely independent of all usefulness to society. The person is primary, not the society; the

State exists for the citizen, not the citizen for the State."

The Christian Church has always insisted that the State has no ultimate and omnipotent authority of its own but derives its authority from God. St. Paul in his epistle to the Romans (xiii, 1) made this clear. "There is no power but of God: the powers that be are ordained by God." This has been the shield under which our forefathers resisted oppression. To quote St. Paul again— the Ruler of the State was the "Minister of God for good," and so long as he fulfilled his high trust it was not right to resist him; but if he forsook it and sought absolute power, then resistance was justified.

THE CASE OF JAMES I

A celebrated instance occurred when James I claimed the right to rule in England as an absolute sovereign. He claimed that he could judge whatever cause he pleased in his own person, free from all risks of prohibition or appeal. He called in aid the authority of Archbishop Bancroft, who declared that it was clear in divinity that he could try cases himself. Such power, said the Archbishop, doubtless belongs to the King by the word of God in the scriptures. But there was a great Lord Chief Justice in those days, Lord Coke, who made it a rule of his life to spend one-fourth of each day in prayer; though I must say I do not know how he managed it, considering the vast amount of other things that he did. Lord Coke told the King that he had no power to try cases himself, and that all cases ought to be determined in a Court of Justice. King James replied: "I always thought and I have often heard the boast that your English law is founded upon reason. If that be so, why have not I and others reason as well as you the judges?" The Lord Chief Justice replied: "True it is, please your Majesty, that God has endowed your Majesty with excellent science as well as great gifts of nature : but your Majesty will allow me to say, with all reverence, that you are not learned in the laws of this your Realm of England . . . which is an art which requires long study and experience before a man can attain to the cognizance of it. The law is the golden met-wand and measure to try the causes of your Majesty's subjects, and it is by that law that your Majesty is protected in safety and peace." King James, in a great rage, said, " Then I am to be under the law—which it is treason to affirm." The Chief Justice replied, " Thus wrote Bracton, ' The King is under no man, save under God and the law.' "

Those words of Bracton quoted by Coke, " The King is under God and the law " epitomise in one sentence the great contribution made by the common lawyers to the Constitution of England. They insisted that the executive power in the land was under the law. In insisting upon this they were really insisting on the Christian principles. If we forget these principles, where shall we finish ? You have only to look to the totalitarian systems of government to see what happens. The society is primary, not the person. The citizen exists for the State, not the State for the citizen. The rulers are not under God and the law. They are a law unto themselves. All law, all courts are simply part of the State machine. The freedom of the individual, as we know it, no longer exists. It is against that terrible despotism, that overwhelming domination of human life, that Christianity has protested with all the energy at its command.

THE PERILS OF INDIVIDUALISM

In noticing, however, the evils of the totalitarian system, let us also remember that individualism has its perils.

The Puritans, who insisted that the King was under God and the law, carried their individualism too far, or, at any rate, some of their successors did. On the one hand they had a great sense of the supreme importance of the individual soul and a vital instinct for setting bounds to the State; but on the other hand they held that there was a natural law which gave every man a right of property in all that he could acquire by his own labour, and once having acquired it, he could amass it, increase it and dispose of it as he willed, without any obligation to account to anybody for his stewardship. The great exponent of this individualism was our own philosopher John Locke, who has had more influence on American thought even than he had on ours. The Constitution of the United States shows one side of the Puritan outlook. It imposes strict limits on the action of those who wield power in the land. The extreme importance attached to the ownership of property in the United States shows another side of Puritanism.

No one doubts now that it is wrong to treat rights of property as sacred. As Sir Ernest Barker has well said, the individualism of the Puritans " based on religion was made to trail clouds of ingloriousness." There have been many people who, having amassed or inherited property, have only too often forgotten that it is only through society that they have acquired it. They have failed to realise that they are under a duty to use it for the benefit of society as a whole and not for their own material advantage. When rights of property are carried to these lengths they are contrary to all Christian teaching. They disregard the high duty of unselfishness. As it is said in the Epistle of St. John, " Whoso hath this world's goods and seeth his brother have need, and shutteth up his compassion from him, how dwelleth the love of God in him ? "

THE INFLUENCE OF CHRISTIANITY

This brings me to the latest and most important influence of Christianity on our law. The preaching of many divines and notably of William Temple brought home the evils of the excessive accumulation of wealth and opportunity in few hands. This has played a considerable part in great changes in the law. The most important, no doubt, have been made by Parliament, which has turned us into a Welfare State which recognises that the State has a duty to secure for every citizen so far as possible full freedom and opportunity for the development of his talents, unhampered by poverty or ill-health. And this action by Parliament has been reflected in decisions of the judges, notably in cases relating to employers and workmen. The courts have repeatedly emphasised the responsibility of employers to provide safe conditions of work for their workmen, and in case of accident to compensate them for their injuries.

But this new state of society has its dangers. It has brought in its train a great increase in the powers of the central government and a lessening in the authority of Parliament and of the courts, so much so that there are fears that the initiative and enterprise of the individual have been hampered too much. We must hope that this danger can be overcome; but it can, I suggest, only be done if we recognise that Christianity is not only a personal religion but also that it has much to teach society itself.

FAMILY LIFE

There is one more subject I must mention, and in some ways it is the most important of all. It is the institution of marriage. The Christian Church has always maintained that marriage is a life-long union, for better or for worse, so long as both shall live.   Divorce was never allowed so as to give the right to remarry.   This principle was in marked contrast to other legal systems such as the Jewish laws or the Roman law, which always permitted divorce to a greater or less extent.   The principle of the indissolubility of marriage was in England for centuries not only the law of the Church but also the law of the land.   It has had a profound influence on the social life of the country.   The family is the primary social unit.   The well-being of the whole community requires that children should, so far as possible, be brought up by their own parents as members of one family, with all the give and take that family life demands, and also with the security that it affords.   The institution of marriage is the legal foundation of this family life.   The principle of indissolubility was the binding force which cemented it.   During the last 96 years the State has abandoned the principle.   Divorce has been allowed for grave causes prescribed by law, but the consequences that were foreseen by the Church, and of which its leaders gave warning, have followed. Undeserving cases have slipped through.   Collusion has not been detected.   The result is that people have come to regard divorce as a matter which can be arranged between the parties.   In so doing, they only too often disregard the interests of their children and pursue their own selfish ends.   Every thinking person is profoundly disturbed by this state of affairs.   It has a grave effect on the family unity and on the national character.   It is almost impossible for the State to retrace its steps so as to make the divorce law more difficult.   The only real remedy is the growth of a strong public opinion condemning divorce, and, I would add, condemning infidelity. It should not be regarded, as it now is, as the private concern of the parties with which no one else has anything to do.   It is the concern of everyone who has the welfare of the country at heart.

CONCLUSION

This brings me to the end.   And what does it all come to?   Surely this, that if we seek truth and justice, we cannot find it by argument and debate, nor by reading and thinking, but only by the maintenance of true religion and virtue.   Religion concerns the spirit in man whereby he is able to recognise what is truth and what is justice; whereas law is only the application, however imperfectly, of truth and justice in our everyday affairs. If religion perishes in the land, truth and justice will also. We have already strayed too far from the faith of our fathers.   Let us return to it, for it is the only thing that can save us.